MW00378493

# THE

# INDEPENDENT FLOOR DEALER SUCCESS SYSTEM

## Make More Money, Work Fewer Hours, & Get Your Life Back

JIM AUGUSTUS ARMSTRONG

Flooring Success Systems
236 South 3rd St., Suite 309
Montrose, CO 81401
1-877-887-5791
Support@FlooringSuccessSystems.com

Image Copyright:
Face palm man: durantelallera/Shutterstock
Rattle snake: anton_novik/Shutterstock

Ordering Information:
For information on quantity purchases by corporations, associations, and others, contact the publisher at the address, email or phone number above.

Independent Floor Dealer Success System: Make More Money, Work Fewer Hours, And Get Your Life Back

By Jim Augustus Armstrong. -- 1st ed.
ISBN: 978-1727741209

# CONTENTS

# ACKNOWLEDGEMENTS

Tiffany Hoeckelman and the team at Lone Orange for their set up and design work which, as always, is fantastic. Susan Trainor for her superb editing. Robert Skrob for his guidance and insights.

And finally, to my wife and business partner, Jolyn. I couldn't have done it without you. Thank you for all you do to make business fun, and our lives an adventure.

# FORWARD BY SCOTT HUMPHREY

I first met Jim Armstrong a few years ago on the last day of Surfaces in Las Vegas. Jim, Scott Perron and I sat around a table in the World Floor Covering Association (WFCA) booth—relaxing after a long and tiring week—and had a lengthy discussion about the state of the flooring industry, it's challenges and opportunities. This was the first time I had a chance to sit down and really get to know Jim. What I sensed was a man who has a passion for the flooring industry, and who cares about helping flooring retailers. It was for this reason that, when he asked me to appear on one of the floor dealer educational webinars he co-hosts for FCNews, I immediately agreed. Since that time, I and the rest of the WFCA leadership have worked with Jim and appeared as guests on webinar events with him multiple times. Over the years I have had the opportunity to get to know Jim better and learn about his mission, which is to help flooring retailers succeed.

There are major challenges facing our industry, not least of which are big box retailers taking market share from independent dealers. There are also incredible opportunities for retailers who are willing to adapt and learn new methods for attracting and keeping customers. Jim has dedicated his career to helping dealers do just that. And Jim has been there to help them thrive and prosper in the 21st Century. This is also my mission, and the reason I joined the WFCA as its CEO. With Jim I have another colleague who is with me on the front lines, equipping retailers to fight the good fight, succeed and prosper.

In our industry there are those who are only concerned with themselves and their own success, and those who are truly interested in helping our industry and giving back. I am happy to say that Jim is one of the latter.

Sincerely,
Scott Humphrey
CEO, World Floor Covering Association

# ICONS

### Case Study

This icon means you're about to read a case study involving a real, live floor dealer using one or more of the strategies taught in this book.

### Rule breaker!

This icon means you're about to get tips and strategies that break commonly followed "rules" of the flooring industry. Pay special attention because breaking these rules will help you get an Unfair Advantage over competitors, beat the boxes, and dramatically increase your profits!

### Watch out!

This icon means you're about to be warned of a deadly pitfall that can hurt your profitability or success.

### What the ...?

This icon means that Jim is about to discuss a commonly held flooring industry belief or practice that's so dumb or harmful to dealers that he gets severely torqued off even thinking about it.

### Run The Numbers

This icon means that Jim is going to show you how much additional revenue a specific strategy can generate for your business.

CHAPTER 1

# JUST IMAGINE HAVING A DAY LIKE THIS

*You drive to your beautiful, well-organized, inviting showroom. You have a big sign out front. Your parking lot is full of cars, and there are customers in your showroom.*

*You walk in at your usual time of 10:00 a.m. and look at the appointment calendar. It's packed with installations, all sold at 45%-50% margins. Your receptionist says that several customers visited this morning wanting to be "squeezed in." But they will have to be squeezed in three weeks from now. Your installers are already booked solid for the next two weeks. The week after that is nearly filled up, too.*

*What a great feeling! You've got reliable staff to handle the day-to-day tasks of running a flooring business. You have well-trained, enthusiastic sales people working with the customers. These customers are perfectly happy paying full margin because your marketing attracts only the customers who buy based on service. Oh, and they're willing to wait in line for a month or more for their installation because they trust you to get their job done right and they only want to work with you.*

*The feast-or-famine cycle doesn't happen anymore because it's all feast.* You have had consistent revenue the last 24 months without huge seasonal swings, enabling you to keep a full-time, consistent team. Plus you have predictable cash flow, as other dealers suffer from their so-called off season. Even when you get an onrush of new customers, you don't panic because you have systems in place to handle all the new business. Your personal workload stays the same. No nights or weekends for you. You use the bump in sales as an opportunity to take your business to the next level. You've gone from being "self-employed" to being a true entrepreneur. You only work Monday through Thursday, so every week you get a three-day weekend.

You look at your calendar to see what's coming up next month, and you smile because you and your spouse are going on a two-week vacation to the Caribbean. It's one of three vacations you'll be taking this year. You remember not long ago when years would go by without a vacation. Now you take plenty of time off to have fun and enjoy life, and while you're away your business continues to run like a well-oiled machine. You don't have to call the office or check business emails when you're on "you" time. When you get back, there's no giant mountain of catch-up work, and your bank balance is higher than before you left.

You lean back in your chair and try to decide what you'd like to do today when you knock off at your usual time of 3:00.

"So, what'll it be this afternoon?" you think. "Golf? The beach? Fishing? Sit on the back deck of my custom home, reading a good book and sipping my favorite beer? Decisions, decisions ..."

Now that's what it's like to have fun being a floor dealer! If you have to drag yourself out of bed in the morning because you hate to go to work, or if you're working like a dog early morning till late at night, you might as well go get a job working for someone else—hell, life's too short to spend it enslaved to your business! Running your own flooring business should be mentally, emotionally, and most of all, financially rewarding, with plenty of time to take off to go out and enjoy life! You don't need to be a marketing expert to make these dreams a reality. All you need are the strategies I cover in this book.

Skeptical? Sounds too good to be true? Think this could never happen for you?

I get it. And I don't blame you if you feel that way. *After* all, it's very, very common for dealers to put in 50 to 70 hours per week, to work weekends, to rarely (or never) take time off for themselves, to be stressed out, to be constantly on the edge of burnout. This state of affairs is epidemic in our industry. Maybe that describes your business. It's all you've known. And you look around you, and most of the dealers you know are the same way.

So yeah, I understand if the life I just described sounds impossible to you right now.

But let me ask you something. As you read about that ideal business and ideal lifestyle, did you feel something down in your gut? Did you find yourself hoping—even a little bit—that maybe, just *maybe*, a life like this might be possible for you?

Because if you did, let me tell you something you may have never been told in your entire career in the flooring industry: It is *possible*. And it's possible for you. Not just other dealers. *You.*

You see, I've helped hundreds of dealers achieve the business and the life they never, ever thought was possible. Some of them had given up on their dreams of a great life, resigning themselves to forever being shackled to a business that ran them ragged. Some were even on the brink of bankruptcy when I met them.

You're going to meet some of those dealers in this book. Dealers like Jerome ...

**CASE STUDY**

## How Jerome Raised His Margins to 50%, Stays Booked Out 12 Weeks, and Got His Life Back!

Jerome Nowowiejski of Brownwood Decorating in Texas is one of my Flooring Success Systems members, and his story should be an inspiration to any dealer who is working too hard for too little, or who thinks that the *Ideal Business* and the *Ideal Lifestyle* I describe above are impossible for a floor dealer. Jerome made an incredible transition in a short period of time, and since learning the strategies I teach, he has a better business as well as a better life. Before I met Jerome, he had extremely low margins, under 30% on residential, yet within only three months of implementing the strategies he was learning from me, he began commanding margins between 45% and 50% on all his residential flooring.

Jerome made an incredible transition in a short period of time, and since learning the strategies I teach, he has a better business as well as a better life. Before I met Jerome, he had extremely low margins, under 30% on residential, yet within only three months of implementing the strategies he was learning from me, he began commanding margins between 45% and 50% on all his residential flooring.

Jerome has had his own flooring store since 2004. Before he put these new systems in place, he says the approach was "Cat and mouse, scratching, trying to get everything you could"; he never left the store, was "worn out ... exhausted."

Jerome values the *Design Audit*™ for identifying the customers you might not want to work with. "It weeds people out because you don't necessarily want to work with everybody," he says. "Perfect example: I had a lady who came in who just ripped me up one side and down the other on price. She came back in a year later ... this was after I had been introduced to Jim Armstrong and started putting his systems in place. She started going through the same thing. So, I said, 'I remember you; you're a returning customer. Let me sit down with you and ask you some questions' ... all her objections just dropped, and by the end of the conversation she was ready to move." That ended up being a $6,000 to $7,000 job at over 40% margins. (*The *Design Audit*™ is my trademarked selling system. You'll learn more about this a little later.)

Jerome was once a slave to his store, working long hours and never taking weekends off. He now regularly takes four-day weekends and several multi-week vacations each year, even travelling out of the country. While he is away, his business continues to run smoothly and make money. He says it's because of my strategies he has put in place: "That's what the *Design Audit*'s for, that's what all the mail-outs that we do before, during, and after the sale are for, that's what our checklist is for."

How's business now? Jerome is normally booked out for two to three months! He considers it "slow" when he's only booked out for two weeks. Why isn't he worried about telling customers they have to wait maybe three months for an installation? "Because most of my customers now are repeat business or referrals," he says. "They're not just coming in off the street." Jerome has also implemented strategies to create total differentiation from competitors, and he's implemented zero-resistance selling strategies. These combine to make prospects completely willing to wait weeks or months for their installation, even if a cheaper-priced competitor can do it that day. Most dealers would be terrified to tell a customer they had to wait three months; it's unthinkable. But that's because they have not implemented the strategies Jerome has. He now has total control over his business and his life. He owns his business, not the other way around.

Jerome now owns seven houses (some for rental income) and another on a lake nearby. All but one is paid off, and he owns his store and warehouse free and clear. Before joining Flooring Success Systems, he only had his own home and one rental property, both with mortgages. By investing the extra profits his business now generates into real estate, Jerome will likely have the option of early retirement if he chooses.

Jerome is proving every day that by implementing the strategies I teach, you can build your *Ideal Business* and live your *Ideal Lifestyle*.

Jerome will be the first to tell you that if he can do it, you can, too. You just need the right systems. And in this book you're going to discover them.

Before we dive into the meat and potatoes, let me ask you ...

# How Many of These "Floor Dealer Dramas" Sound Familiar?

*Check any that apply.*

## Sales & Marketing

❑ **Online marketing feels so overwhelming that even thinking about it sets your teeth on edge.** Every online "expert" is saying you should be doing something different. It seems like there are dozens of things you're "supposed" to do online. Who has the time to figure this stuff out ... or even wants to? But you know you've got to get your online marketing dialed in because that's where your customers are. (Help!)

❑ **You'd like to have a reliable, consistent way of attracting quality customers week-in and week-out.** No cheap-price gimmicks or "free installation" come-ons that just attract low-value price shoppers. Just honest work for honest customers who are willing to pay more for quality products, service, and craftsmanship.

❑ **You've got a great OFFLINE reputation,** but you don't have enough online reviews (or too many negative ones), so your ONLINE reputation is suffering.

❑ **You've got a very successful flooring business,** but you're always on the lookout for new strategies to make you even more successful.

❑ **Competitors or jerk customers have left fake negative reviews online.** They're a big, black mark on your reputation; they're untrue, but the people reading them are judging you based on false reviews. You don't know what to do about it.

❏ **Your sales team only closes three out of 10 walk-ins (which is the national average).** This means 70% DON'T buy. So, 70% of all the money you spent in advertising and overhead to get people into your store is wasted. Not to mention the hours upon hours thrown away on price shoppers who use you for information, then walk out and buy from some box store. You've heard of dealers with close rates of 50%, 60%, even 70% or more, but you don't know how to make it happen in your business. (Or maybe you don't believe it's possible in your community.)

❏ **It seems like there are 20 social media platforms you should be on, with a new one popping up every other week.** You don't have time to keep up with all of it. You'd like a simple, straightforward social media strategy that works on auto-pilot, that actually produces customers and leaves you free to focus on what's more important.

❏ **You feel stuck charging 30% margins for residential remodel jobs.** This is razor thin, creates cash-flow problems, and makes it nearly impossible to pay for quality help. 45% margins would be life-changing. You know of other dealers who charge this much, but you're in a competitive market and you're worried you'll lose customers if you raise your prices.

❏ **You know you should be marketing to your past customers regularly** so you can get their repeat business and referrals to their friends and relatives. But you keep putting it off because you're not sure how to go about it and you don't have the time to figure it out.

❏ **You want to do more to market your business, but so many of the things you've tried have been a stupid waste of time and money.** You're willing to invest to grow, but jeez ... you need something that's PROVEN to work at attracting customers.

❑ **You're tired of the empty promises and hype of ad reps,** lead generation companies, website companies, social media companies, online "experts," and all the other sales vultures calling and emailing you every day to take your money and sell you crap that doesn't work for flooring dealers.

## Competitors

❑ **There used to be such a thing as customer loyalty.** But now you keep losing customers to box stores offering "free" installation or other cheap-price gimmicks.

❑ **You watch another customer walk out the door** because your estimate is $200 higher than the guy down the street.

❑ **You drive by your competitor's store, and you get that queasy feeling because their parking lot is packed full of cars.** Then you notice that one of the cars belongs to someone you thought was a loyal past customer. You reach for the Alka-Seltzer.

❑ **Box stores and national dealers are everywhere you look on TV, radio, the internet**—not to mention all over your town. They are spending millions of dollars in advertising to create massive brand awareness and to steal your customers. You can't come close to matching their ad budgets, so you're eager to find cost-effective ways to fight back ... and win.

❑ **You're tired of the copycat, me-too advertising in flooring,** but your website and other advertising looks too much like your competition's. No differentiation. You KNOW you're different, dammit! And you would like an effective, proven way to communicate this so that customers "get it" and buy from you, even if you're more expensive.

- ❑ **Chuck in a truck.** These are jobbers who operate out of their truck, with low or no overhead and charge next to nothing to steal jobs! You get pinched in the middle, with big boxes outspending you on one end, and low-priced jobbers spending nothing on the other end.

## Lifestyle & Business Management

- ❑ **You've spent years (decades?) building your business.** The dreams of a better life are what have kept you burning the midnight oil all these years. But the "dream" hasn't happened, and you're starting to feel like you're running on a hamster wheel— lots of energy expended, but no forward motion.

- ❑ **You're making a lot of money, your business is growing, but it has too much control over your life.** You're putting in way more hours than you'd like in order to feed the beast. This has caused you to neglect hobbies you enjoy. Your physical fitness is suffering. You rarely take vacations, and you don't get enough time with your family. You'd like to have a successful business AND get your life back.

- ❑ **You and your staff do an outstanding "technical" job of providing quality flooring and installations—your customers love you.** But you need more of the knowledge, skills, savvy, and expertise to properly market and manage what you do.

- ❑ **You missed your daughter's dance recital** (or soccer game or school play) because you had to work late ... again.

- ❑ **You want something more out of life than work, work, work, work, and more work.** But you don't know how to get there.

- ❑ **You love the flooring business, but** ... you're feeling burned out from all the long hours, nights, and weekends.

- ❑ **You've resigned yourself to working 60-plus hours per week,** and never being able to take a two-week vacation because if you leave for that long, things start falling apart. You have come to expect that it is just the nature of the flooring business.

❏ **You can't quite put your finger on it, but deep down inside you know something's wrong.** You get up, go to work, come home, eat, watch TV, go to bed, then do it all again. Wash, rinse, repeat. You don't really talk about it, but you're wondering if this is all life has to offer. Secretly you're desperate for something more.

If any of these sound familiar ... you are not alone. Every single challenge mentioned above came from a floor dealer I have worked with to help them solve it.

If any of these problems hit a little too close to home ... you are in the right place. My team and I have helped hundreds of dealers overcome all of these challenges. All of them.

Every.

Single.

One.

I can help you, too. And in the pages of this book, you are going to find the answers. I promise.

But I need something from you. Your commitment. Your commitment that for the hour or so that it takes to read this book, you'll keep an open mind to NEW strategies and NEW ways of doing things. Because if you aren't open to the new, then you're stuck with the old. And where has the old gotten you?

Exactly.

So, here's the deal. I'll give you the very best I have to offer to help you make a lot more money, work less, get your life back, and beat the boxes. And you agree to keep an open mind while you read this book.

Deal?

Okay, let's jump in.

JIM AUGUSTUS ARMSTRONG

CHAPTER 2

# WHY BIG BOXES HAVE KILLED SO MANY RETAILERS AND HOW YOU CAN COMPETE AND WIN

Most flooring dealers are running on a hamster wheel, trying to run faster and faster, trying to build their businesses. It can seem like a cruel, never-ending marathon. One month you have customers coming in, you have enough money to cover costs—hell, some months you have more work than you can handle. You're planning your next vacation with your family, and life is good. But then a month or two later, your work slows down and you're stressed about where all the flooring jobs have disappeared to. Your sales have evaporated, and your cash flow hits critical. So, you run even harder, putting in 50, 60, even 70 hours per week, working more to make the same or less. You're overworked and stressed out. Or even worse, you wind up closing your doors like so many other dealers have.

This is the fear that keeps too many dealers awake at night.

Even dealers who have growing businesses still find themselves working too many hours, stressed out, worried about the competition, and not able to enjoy the lifestyle they've always dreamed of. They feel like slaves to their stores.

To make matters worse, box stores are gobbling up more and more of the flooring market. Honest, hardworking, independent dealers like you are being attacked by these billion-dollar corporations that want to bury you. They don't give a damn if your business was started by your grandfather and has been in your family for three generations. Look at what they did to local lumberyards; there used to be as many lumberyards in each town as McDonald's. Now the lumberyards are gone, victims of the big boxes. And unless you act now, your flooring dealership could be next.

Big boxes only care about one thing: hitting their numbers for Wall Street. This way they get their fat multimillion-dollar bonuses. If your business dies in their pursuit of revenue ... well, too damn bad.

Apply for a job and get an apron.

They've already done it to a long list of other retail categories, and now they're gunning for you. They figure it will be like shooting fish in a barrel.

But they didn't count on something: **Some of those fish have teeth ... and they bite!**

You see, I've dedicated my career to arming dealers like you with the tools to fight back and kick the boxes—hard—where it hurts. By growing your flooring dealership.

So let me ask you: *What if you didn't have to run on the hamster wheel of doom anymore?* What if you could beat the boxes and create a foundation for your business that brings great customers, who are happy to pay higher prices, day-in and day-out, so you never have to worry about cash flow again?

What if you could transform your flooring business so it allows you to live a great life—working less than 35 hours per week, taking vacations, and creating amazing memories with your family? Leaving a legacy behind. And what if all this could be built by using a simple, three-step system? In this book you're going to learn how lots of other dealers just like you have done it, and how you can, too.

14

**Watch Out!**

### How "Spray and Pray" Is Killing Your Ability to Get New Customers

It seems like every other day a new social media platform or digital advertising strategy emerges that the experts say you must be doing in order to succeed. I call this the "spray and pray" approach, where you try a bunch of different strategies and pray one of them works.

You don't need a spray and pray approach. You need a system for getting a steady, year-round stream of jobs that's been proven to work for hundreds of other dealers in every type of market, that you can simply plug into your business and let it bring you only the very best customers. Let's rid your life of spending time with price shoppers, and let's get out of the "bid business" where you visit homes all over your market area, give prices, and listen to someone tell you the latest "free installation" offer they got from some big box. Instead, allow me to reveal the opportunity for a new and better life as a flooring dealer. No more hustle, just honest work with honest customers. I'm going to reveal the three—and only three—proven steps that will give you the biggest results, in the shortest time, for the least money.

## Why Should You Listen to Me?

Since 2007, I've been helping floor dealers make more, work less, and get their lives back. I've dedicated my business and my career to helping floor dealers succeed, and since 2007, more than 2,000 dealers have relied on me for marketing training to help them make more money while working less.

Our ground breaking, proprietary floor dealership growth methodology—The Flooring Success System—helps floor dealers generate lots of new customers and increase profits, all while working fewer hours. It's revolutionizing the way flooring business owners everywhere are growing their businesses.

## WHAT DEALERS ARE SAYING

 *"Our revenue is up 79.3% over last year! Thanks, Jim!"*
*– Mike Phoenix, Connecticut*

 *"I'm working less than 35 hours per week, revenue is up 50% ... business is fun again!" – Earl Swalm, Saskatchewan*

 *"I made an extra $90,463 in one month using Jim's strategies." – David Kocian, Texas*

These dealers—and others you're going to meet in this book—experienced these results because they made some simple shifts in the way they approach their businesses. Here's what I mean ...

CHAPTER 3

# A SIMPLE 3-STEP SYSTEM THAT WILL TRANSFORM HOW YOU GET AND KEEP CUSTOMERS

## How Transitioning From "Hunter" to "Rancher" Will Save Your Business and Your Life

Most dealers are hunters, meaning they are transaction oriented. They spend their time, energy, and money hunting down the next customer, bagging it, skinning it, and then they're off hunting for the next one. There are three big problems with hunting:

**First,** hunting is very, very hard work. Sometimes you get the game, and other times you go home with nothing. Dealers try to get good at hunting, but in reality customers hate being hunted. Just like wild game, they have a natural fear of the hunter. So, they do the only logical thing they can think of—price shopping and beating you up about how some box store with Chuck in the truck is offering free installation.

**Second,** hunting is unpredictable. One day there's game everywhere and you've got all the customers you need. The next day they disappear like a fart in the wind. Your showroom is empty, your phone is growing cobwebs, and you're wondering where all the game went.

**Third,** hunting keeps you stuck on the hamster wheel. You work more and more hours hunting down customers, driving all over looking at houses, measuring and giving out prices, only to make the same or less. If you do manage to grow, hunting takes so much time and energy that it's hard to enjoy it. You're working so darn many hours that you're stressed out and burned out.

Ranching changes all that. A rancher's job is to round up a small herd of customers who keep him or her living in style. There are three big benefits to ranching:

**First,** ranching is very, very easy compared to hunting.

**Second,** ranching is predictable. When your herd of customers is rounded up and fenced in, you don't have to wonder where your next customer is coming from.

**Third,** ranching lets you escape the hamster wheel of doom. You work fewer and fewer hours, and your income goes up and up.

## How Dealers Are Transforming Their Businesses With a Simple 3-Step System

So, how have the dealers profiled in this book transitioned from hunter to rancher? By using the three-step *Flooring Success System.* We've helped hundreds of dealers from across the U.S. and Canada transition from the stress of the hunter to the peace of mind of the rancher. I'm going to teach you the three core steps to this process; *Before, During, and After.* I'll walk you through the entire *Before, During, and After* system so you can start putting it in place right away, beginning today. Figure 3.1 illustrates the BDA system. Let's break it down.

**The first step is *Before*.** This is what you do to round up new customers before they've done business with you. *Before* are your marketing efforts to attract new customers before they have purchased from you. There are

hundreds of advertising strategies that dealers use to try and get new customers to call or visit. The choices seem endless, and it can get pretty overwhelming and confusing. Good news! In this book we are going to simplify things and look at the only three online strategies you need to attract the best new customers from the internet. No more overwhelm.

Figure 3.1

**The second step, *During*,** is what you do during the sales process to get customers to buy from you instead of your competition. It gets you out of the "proposal business," spending all your days and nights preparing and delivering proposals to customers who don't buy from you. Instead, this step shows you how to get high-quality customers to say "yes," so you can give out fewer proposals and get more sales.

**Then it's time for the third step, *After*.** This is what you do after the sale to dramatically increase your repeat and referral business. It gets you your customers' next projects in a competition-free zone, and gets you referrals to their friends and family. You do this by using a strategic outreach and messaging process that delivers an ongoing stream of repeat customers and referrals. This is where you supercharge your results because you learn how to stay connected with your herd of past customers in a very personal way, building real relationships so you can generate a consistent stream of sales week in and week out. Many dealers I've worked with have totally transformed their businesses using just this one step.

## Why Most Floor Dealer Advertising Sucks

To be honest, I hate much of the advertising and marketing strategies being taught to floor dealers, especially digital marketing. I see dealers getting barraged every day with phone calls, emails, and drop-ins trying to get them to buy website services, SEO, online directory listings, social media, online leads, pay-per-click, and on and on. You get harassed by all these internet sales vultures trying to suck you dry with monthly and annual fees, with zero accountability for generating real, paying customers. Too many dealers spend their money and their time doing crap that doesn't generate sales (or only gets mediocre results, or only attracts price shoppers), and I'm sick of it. I've been railing against it for a decade.

**Watch Out!**  **Beware of Lead Generation Companies**

A recent business article reports that HomeAdvisor is being sued by a group of eight (severely pissed off) home-improvement companies. Here are just two of the several allegations:

- *The leads sold to the companies are "overwhelmingly bogus" and "illusory" because they are often "over distributed" or contain, among other things, disconnected phone numbers, people who are not homeowners, or contacts for nonexistent residences.*

- *When companies cancel their HomeAdvisor membership, HomeAdvisor leaves their company profile page on its website, and sells the information entered by individuals who attempt to contact the company to other HomeAdvisor members.*

I've been saying for years that instead of buying leads from HomeAdvisor, you'd be better off heaping your money into a

**Continued:**

pile, setting it on fire, and roasting marshmallows over it. That way you'd get at least some use out of your hard-earned dollars.

All joking aside, this angers me. And it should you, too. Dealers are working their asses off trying to build their businesses, trying to compete against boxes and other billion-dollar multinational corporations that want to crush them. They're working 60-plus hours a week to put food on the table and support their families.

And then these advertising bloodsuckers come along and promise dealers tons of leads, sucking them dry with their monthly fees, with zero accountability. And deliver nothing in return. And even actively attempt to rip you off.

Bastards.

And HomeAdvisor isn't the only one. You might be thinking that buying leads from Angie's List might be a safer bet. Think again. Angie's List was acquired by HomeAdvisor in October 2017, and faces its own legal challenges. Angie's List just settled a class-action lawsuit for $1.4 million for manipulating search results and reviews.

None of this is at all surprising to me. Over the last 10 years, I've spoken with many floor dealers who have bought leads from various lead generation companies, and the results are rarely good. For example, one dealer I spoke with recently was spending $6,000 per month buying leads. Twelve months and $72,000 later, he had wound up with mostly price shoppers. He didn't even break even. $72,000 down the drain. Unfortunately, I've heard various versions of his story from many different dealers.

Look, you need a reliable, proven way to get great customers day in and day out, and skip all the bullshit. Then you can tell HomeAdvisor and any other sales vultures who call to pound sand.

I made up my mind from the beginning that I would never work that way. I've dedicated my career to providing dealers like you with proven strategies that *actually produce results*. And now I am finally revealing the three-step system that generates 90% of the customers for flooring dealers. That is why I'm not interested in keeping this information to myself or just for select clients. It's become my mission to get my system into the hands of as many floor dealers as possible because I truly hate seeing so many great flooring businesses trapped on the hamster wheel of doom. You deserve to enjoy a great lifestyle. That's why in this book I'm giving you the tools to start putting this system in place.

## 3 Deadly Mistakes Keeping Dealers Trapped on the Hamster Wheel of Doom

Here are the three mistakes I see floor dealers making all the time that destroy any chance of getting off the hamster wheel.

## Mistake #1

The first mistake is that dealers don't put *Before, During, and After* together into a system. Most dealers are weak in at least one or two of these. For example, many dealers spend tens of thousands of dollars on their *Before* strategies—on advertising to get prospects to visit their stores. Some dealers do a fairly good job with this, and they generate a decent number of walk-ins, but most walk-ins don't buy. In fact, studies show that the average dealer only closes three out of 10 walk-ins. So, dealers are spending thousands and thousands of dollars in advertising, but 70% of that money is going to waste. This is because they are weak in the *During* part of the system. They don't have a strong system for converting a customer visit into a job, so they lose most of their potential customers.

To make matters worse, customers who do buy never receive consistent, ongoing communication from the dealer *After* the sale. So, what happens? These customers get poached by the boxes and other competitors. The dealer loses all that repeat business and their referrals because they have no *After* system in place.

So, if you're weak in any of the three areas—*Before, During, or After*—you have gigantic holes in your fence, and your customers are being poached by your competition.

## Mistake #2

The second mistake is not developing a great online reputation by using reviews. Getting reviews is a *Before* strategy because it's something you do to attract new customers BEFORE they purchase from you. Nowadays, reviews are absolutely critical for getting new customers. Over 90% of consumers read reviews before visiting a local business, and 88% of them trust reviews as much as a referral.

I've discovered that many dealers who have a great offline reputation have a lousy online reputation. Here's an example:

**CASE STUDY**

## This Dealer Is Toiling Away In The Estimate Business

Kevin is a dealer from Colorado, and he's upset because he's getting up every day trying to build his business and he's getting his head handed to him on a stick by the boxes because he's got hardly any reviews, and half of them are bad. He goes out and measures homes, and puts together estimates, spending hours and hours of his time. And he can't figure out why he's only closing three out of 10 prospects. He's working in the "estimate" business instead of in the flooring business. Why is this happening? Because he doesn't realize that within 30 seconds of leaving the house, Mrs. Prospect picks up her smartphone and within three clicks finds him online, sees his 2.6 star rating, and BOOM ... he's off the list. (Or he never gets called to do an estimate in the first place.) And all the work, all the hours invested, all the advertising money spent—it's all for nothing because he doesn't have this simple thing taken care of: *his ONLINE reputation.*

## Mistake #3

Finally, the third mistake we see is that the vast majority of dealers totally ignore their past customers. Flooring is a relationship business, and if you want to maximize your success you've got to build deep, long-lasting relationships with your past customers. Regular communication with your customers is what you do *After* the sale to generate repeat and referral business and to lock them in an iron cage away from competitors. The *After* step is critical because box stores are lurking in every city and everywhere online, spending millions of dollars in advertising to poach your customers from you.

The *After* step works by using a strategic outreach and messaging process that generates an ongoing stream of repeat customers and referrals to your door. Most flooring dealers get as much repeat business from their customers as funeral homes. After all, they have the hunter mindset; after getting a customer, they've moved on to the next.

Ranchers take a completely different approach that makes all the difference, and I'll go into this in detail later in this book.

Dealers in my exclusive marketing program have doubled and tripled their revenue by implementing an *After* strategy and incorporating messages using the 90/10 formula. (I'll explain how this formula works in Chapter 6.) This gets you off the boom and bust roller coaster and replaces it with the peace of mind of a steady stream of honest clients year-round.

CHAPTER 4

# BEFORE: HOW TO ATTRACT A STEADY STREAM OF THE BEST NEW CUSTOMERS

The *Before* step includes all your marketing and advertising strategies to attract customers before they ever do business with you. We're going to look at three strategies for communicating with consumers online so you build trust, create total differentiation from competitors, and round up a herd of the best customers from the internet.

Flooring is unique. It's not like any other retail product. Marketing that works for a plumber or a roofer won't necessarily work to sell flooring. It makes me angry when all the digital "marketing companies" that don't know anything about our industry try to sell floor dealers generic stuff that wastes a dealer's money. Too many dealers hire a teenager or a relative to set up their site, or overpay for some generic template built by someone who is more interesting in getting their money than in making sure the dealer's business grows with new customers.

So, I went on a quest to figure out exactly what is and what *isn't* the truth about online marketing. With my access to experts in the flooring industry, and the people I know at distributors, manufacturers, and associations—not to mention the work I've done with hundreds of dealers—I've been able to identify which online strategies really work for getting customers, and which don't. We've built, tested, and proven these strategies and put them to work for dealers, and here I'm pulling back the curtain so you can put them to work in your business.

Now, every consumer who goes online searching for flooring has an unspoken question on his or her mind: *Why should I buy from you instead of your competitor?* Most dealers don't do a very good job answering this question. These strategies are going to help you answer this unspoken question in a powerful way that makes you the overwhelmingly obvious choice, and rounds up a herd of really great customers.

## Before Strategy #1: Attract the Best Customers Online With the 5-Star Review System

**CASE STUDY** — **This Dealer Was Down for the Count**

Matt Capell bought Capell Flooring & Interiors in 2008. At that time the business grossed $2 million, but the margins averaged 20%. Like many dealers, the recession hit Matt very hard, and in 2010, he only grossed $400,000. (This was due in part to all the contractors filing bankruptcy and stiffing Matt's company on what they owed.)

This was an incredibly stressful and scary time for Matt and his wife. In fact, things got so bad that they considered closing the business.

So, he made a decision. Matt began looking for the cheapest ways to market his business in an attempt to turn things around.

His store location is not highly visible because it's not on a major road or highway. He tracked where his customers were coming from and found that he got them in three primary ways: 1) repeat customer, 2) referral, and 3) online. In fact, most of his new customers were finding him online.

So, Matt began dialing in on his online review system, using the same strategies contained in this book. As a result he brought his business back from the brink, and now he is making more money than ever before. Check out what Matt said about his turnaround:

"The recession hit us hard. By 2010 our revenue was down to $400,000, and my wife and I were considering closing the doors. I began using the online strategies Jim teaches, and it literally saved my business. Last year we did $2 million at 40% margins." – Matt Capell, Idaho

Figure 4.1

27

In Figure 4.1 you can see that Matt has more than 120 positive reviews and a 5-star rating. His online reputation is so powerful it blows away his competitors, including the box stores. His reviews position him as the overwhelmingly obvious choice in his market, and answer the unspoken question: Why should I choose you instead of your competitors? My goal for you is to do the same for your store.

Here's why getting a steady stream of positive online reviews is so critical in today's market if you want to beat the boxes and attract great customers:

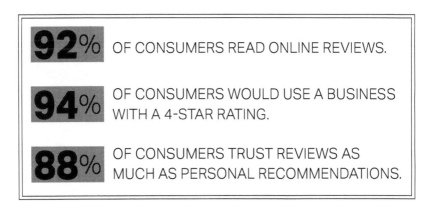

This means that having great online reviews is like having another stream of referrals coming into your business.

Also, 73% of consumers think that reviews older than 3 months are no longer relevant, which is why it's important that you're continuously getting new reviews.

Figure 4.2 illustrates the 5-Star Review System. Let's break it down:

28

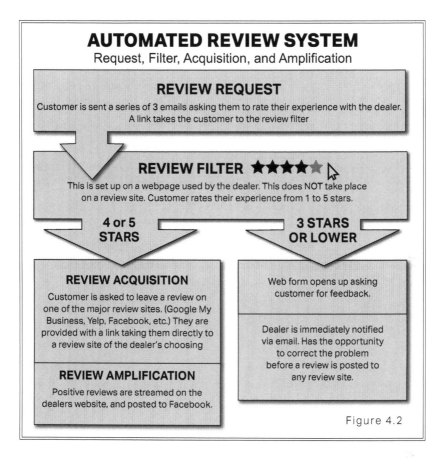

Figure 4.2

**Step 1: review request.** An effective method for requesting reviews that we implement for dealers is a three-step email campaign. After the installation, each customer gets a series of three emails, which go out on day 1, day 3, and day 7. Each email contains a link taking the customer to the review filter. (Sending review requests via email is how Matt got most of his reviews.)

**Step 2: review filtering.** The customer clicks the link in the review request email. She is taken to a web page used by the dealer, and has the opportunity to rate her experience from 1 to 5 stars. This does NOT take place on a review site. This is important because you might get a customer who is unhappy with your service, and you don't want to send her to a review site until you've had a chance to correct the problem.

If the customer gives a rating of 3 stars or lower, an online form opens up where she can leave feedback on what caused her to be less than 100% satisfied. The dealer is notified immediately via email of negative ratings so steps can be taken to correct the problem and turn an unsatisfied customer into a raving fan.

Competitors or jerk customers can still go directly to the review sites and leave fake negative reviews. This problem is solved with the next step.

**Step 3: review acquisition.** When a customer gives one of our dealers a 4- or 5-star rating in the review filter, the customer sees a message inviting her to leave a review on one of the major review sites such as Google My Business, Facebook, Houzz, Yelp, etc. A link in the message takes the customer directly to the review site of the dealer's choosing. I recommend driving customers to the sites where you are most in need of reviews. If you don't have any reviews at all, start with Google My Business.

Getting lots of positive reviews also protects you against fake negative reviews left by competitors or jerk customers. Let's say that on Google you've got 50 great reviews. It won't matter if you get some fake 1-star reviews. Your average star rating will experience little to no change. Also, consumers realize that even the best companies get negative comments occasionally. As long as you've got lots of positive comments, a few negative ones won't hurt you.

**Step 4: review amplification.** The 4- and 5-star reviews are streamed on our dealers' websites as they are posted. Every time a prospect visits a dealer's site, he or she sees an ongoing stream of new, positive reviews from all over the internet. These reviews are also posted on the dealer's Facebook page.

Google likes reviews. Setting up review acquisition and amplification will help the best customers find you online.

Not only will the 5-Star Review System generate lots of customers for you, it will help you command higher prices. Here's what Matt said about that:

## CASE STUDY

### My Customers Tell Me I'm the Most Expensive

"My customers regularly tell me I'm way higher than other estimates, and they still buy from me. I just bid a $60,000 job, and the next highest bidder was $8,000 lower. I got the job. My online reviews are a big part of why I'm able to sell at prices higher than my competitors."
*– Matt Capell*

You see, having dozens of great reviews answers the unspoken question so powerfully that Matt is able to sell in a competition-free zone.

## RUN THE NUMBERS

Let's say your average ticket is $3,000, and by having 50 to 100 positive online reviews you are able to generate only one additional sale per week that you wouldn't have otherwise gotten (a conservative number).

Average ticket: $3,000

1 extra sale per week x 52 weeks = $156,000

That's $156,000 in additional revenue.

## Before Strategy #2: How to Turn Your Website Into a Customer Capture System

Recently Synchrony Financial and GE Financial did studies of the path to purchase consumers take when buying big-ticket items of $500 or more. Figure 4.3 illustrates the results of these studies.

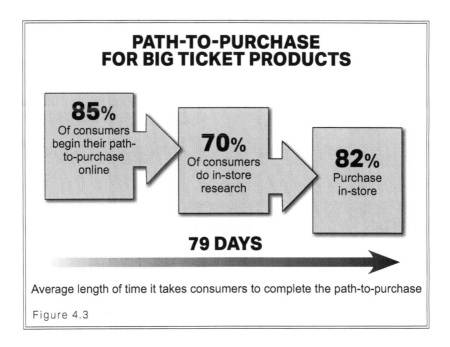

**PATH-TO-PURCHASE FOR BIG TICKET PRODUCTS**

**85%** Of consumers begin their path-to-purchase online

**70%** Of consumers do in-store research

**82%** Purchase in-store

**79 DAYS**

Average length of time it takes consumers to complete the path-to-purchase

Figure 4.3

85% of consumers begin their path to purchase online. 70% do in-store research. And 83% purchase in a bricks-and-mortar store. This entire process takes 79 days.

Therefore, the goal of your website is to do three things:

- **First,** answer the unspoken question. *(Why should I choose you instead of your competitors?)*

- **Second,** have a strong call to action.

- **Third,** capture each visitor's contact information so you can do follow-up marketing and stay in front of prospects throughout the 79-day path to purchase.

Most flooring websites don't do a good job with these three things. Here's what I mean ...

## Walk a Mile in Cathy Consumer's Shoes

The first thing we need to do is put ourselves in the shoes of someone shopping for flooring.

Meet Cathy Consumer. Cathy is excited to get new floors. Her current floors are dated and worn out, and she can't wait to replace them.

But she's also nervous. She doesn't know anything about flooring, and she's worried that she'll spend $8,000 on new floors and wind up with a decision she'll regret. Also, her sister-in-law recently bought from a dealer who did a shoddy installation and never repaired it. So, she's also worried she'll get stuck with an incompetent or dishonest dealer.

Let's follow Cathy online as she tries to find an answer to her unspoken question: *Why should I choose you instead of your competitors?*

Cathy googles flooring in her city and pulls up four websites. The first site has the name of the dealer at the top, links to products they sell, and contact information. So she goes to the next site, and it says the same thing: business name, links to products, and contact information. The third site says the same thing: business name, links to products, and contact information. I call sites that follow this formula "name, rank, and serial number" sites. There's a gigantic problem with these kinds of sites. Even though they might look very professional, they don't answer the unspoken question: *Why should I choose you instead of your competitors?* That's because they are all saying the same thing: here's our name, here's what we sell, here's how to find us.

Then Cathy visits the website of Frank, a dealer using Flooring Success Systems, and sees this ad (Figure 4.4):

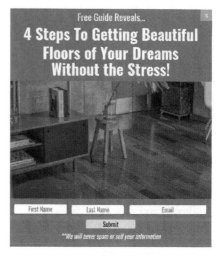

She gives her contact information and gets the guide. Now Frank is able to stay in front of Cathy during her 79-day path to purchase with emails specifically designed to answer the unspoken question: *Why should I choose you instead of your competitors?*

This one strategy has allowed Frank to easily accomplish all

Figure 4.4

three goals for his website without having to make major changes to his site.

- **First,** he's answered the unspoken question in Cathy's mind. The Consumer's Guide overwhelmingly answers this question by giving Cathy over a dozen compelling reasons why she should choose Frank's store.

- **Second,** he's got a strong call to action, which is to download the Consumer's Guide.

- **Third,** he's captured Cathy's contact information so he can stay in front of her during the 79-day path to purchase.

Every few days she will receive an email from Frank educating her on how to choose a dealer, and re-answering the unspoken question. Frank is with her each step of the way during her 79-day path to purchase, building trust and confidence with her. When Cathy is ready to buy, who do you think she's going to choose?

I can tell you that it's virtually guaranteed that no other dealer has a system like this in Frank's market, so he's got an enormous competitive advantage

## $200,000 Extra Per Year

Matt Capell uses the Consumer's Guide as his customer capture system for his website, but he also hands out printed copies to every person who walks into his store. The guide positions Matt as a Trusted Advisor, and gives powerful answers to the unspoken question: *Why should I buy from you instead of your competitors?* So, when someone leaves without buying so they can shop elsewhere, the guide will often bring this customer back. Here's what Matt had to say:

**"I'm generating around $200,000 per year using Jim's lead capture and Consumer's Guide." – Matt Capell**

---

### RUN THE NUMBERS

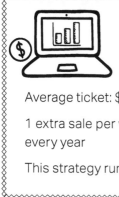 Let's say the lead capture, 79-day follow-up, and Consumer's Guide generate a mere one additional sale per week that you wouldn't have otherwise gotten.

Average ticket: $3,000

1 extra sale per week x 52 weeks = $156,000 in extra revenue every year

This strategy runs in the background, so it's like free money.

---

## Before Strategy #3: The Facebook Customer Generator

There are dozens of social media platforms, and it seems like a new one pops up every week. Figure 4.6 illustrates why I'm focusing on Facebook:

Right now, 68% of Americans are on Facebook. This dwarfs the number on Twitter, Instagram, Pinterest, and LinkedIn. This doesn't make those other platforms bad, or suggest that you shouldn't use them. But I want to focus on strategies that will give you the biggest results, in the shortest time, for the least hassle and money. Since Facebook is where the majority of your customers are hanging out, you need to be there, too. If and when another platform becomes more effective for dealers than Facebook, we'll adjust tactics. But for now that's still the place to be.

**SOCIAL MEDIA # USERS IN THE U.S.**

**68**% of Americans are on FACEBOOK

**21**% TWITTER

**28**% INSTAGRAM

**26**% PINTEREST

**25**% LINKEDIN

---

*Every Facebook post should do one or more of the following:*

- Attract followers

- Create engagement

- Get customers OFF Facebook and into your store (or on the phone with you)

---

A big mistake I see dealers make is they publish posts that don't do these three specific jobs, so they get lousy results. We manage Facebook marketing for our Flooring Success Systems members, and we do a dozen different kinds of posts and strategies to accomplish these three things. Figures 4.7, 4.8, and 4.9 are posts from one of the Facebook strategies we implement for floor dealers.

These are posts promoting the Consumer's Guide. When a customer sees these, she clicks on the link in the post, which takes her to an opt-in page where she gets the guide. She is then subscribed to the 79-day email sequence I discussed earlier.

This turns your Facebook page into another Customer Capture system, it answers the unspoken question, and it gets people off Facebook and into your store. Flooring Success Systems members have access to the Consumer's Guide. If you're not a member yet, you can use your own free offer. Make sure it's compelling and valuable enough that people are willing to give you their contact info in exchange.

We also boost the posts for our dealers so they get better reach. The cost to do this is very low, but it generates much better results.

Figure 4.7

Figure 4.8

Figure 4.9

## RUN THE NUMBERS

Let's say the Facebook strategy only generates four sales per month.

Average ticket: $3,000

4 extra sales per month x 12 months = $156,000 in extra revenue

Considering the low cost, this is an incredible return on investment.

CHAPTER 5

# DURING: HOW TO STOP GIVING OUT PROPOSALS AND INSTEAD CLOSE MORE SALES

Most dealers are in the "proposal" business. Studies have shown that if 10 people walk into a floor dealership, the average dealer only closes three of them. That's dismal. Dealers are spending a fortune, not to mention a lot of time and energy, getting people to walk in their door or call, but 70% of that money and time is wasted.

This happens because dealers are weak in the *During* step. By fixing this step, you can dramatically increase your revenue without increasing your ad spend. Let's say you're only closing three out of 10 walk-ins. If you simply increase that to four out of 10, you've just grown your revenue by 33% without spending another dime in advertising.

**Watch Out!**

**If You Don't Have a System for *Selling*, You'll Always Be at the Mercy of Your Customer's System for *Buying***

And your customer's system for buying is to shop you. She'll come into your dealership, waste hours of your valuable time, and then buy from Home Depot. She'll use you for advice, and then turn around and buy online from Empire. How does it feel to have your time totally abused by customers?

If you want to make more while working less, you've got to have a strong *During* step in place so that you control the sales process. The *During* step that we teach dealers is our *Design Audit*™ sales system.

## Benefits of the *Design Audit*

1. Gives you total control of the process from the second a customer walks in your door.
2. Quickly weeds out tire-kicking, price-shopping "bottom feeders."
3. Positions you as a Trusted Advisor, like the family doctor.
4. Creates total differentiation from your competitors.
5. Increases your average ticket size.
6. Answers the unspoken question on every consumer's mind: Why should I do business with you instead of your competitor?
7. Causes customers to independently arrive at the conclusion: "I'd have to be a complete idiot to buy from anyone else, even if they're half the price."
8. It's brain-dead easy for a newbie salesperson to learn quickly, even if he or she has zero experience in the flooring business.
9. Enables you to command margins of 45%-50% or more.
10. Increases your sales *without* increasing advertising costs.

## This Dealer Loves Home Depot

Dealers using the *Design Audit* are happy to have Home Depot as a neighbor. They know that Home Depot will lure "shoppers" into the area. Many of those shoppers visit these dealers' stores, and their Sales Closer System switches "shoppers" to "buyers." Home Depot actually generates sales for these dealers! Like they do for Mark ...

"We love having Home Depot as our neighbor! We take a lot of business from them!" – Mark, Illinois (That's him in the photo.)

Many of the dealers I work with are within a couple of miles of a Home Depot or other box store. Some are literally right across the street. They don't care. They love taking business from them, too!

Mike, a dealer from Connecticut, increased his year-over-year revenue by 79% by introducing several new sales and marketing strategies into his business. Implementing the *Design Audit* was a big part of the mix.

The vast majority of flooring sales people have not been given a step-by-step sales process that walks prospects down a logical path from "shopper" to "buyer." They haven't been trained in a process that can be learned, measured for results, and where they can be held accountable for results. As a result, most sales people wing it. This leaves far too much to chance, especially if you want to close more sales and command high margins.

Let's look at the four steps of the *Design Audit* selling system.

## Step 1: How to Take Control of the Sales Process

When a customer walks into a flooring store, most sales people make a critical mistake in the first 30 seconds that virtually guarantees they will get beat up on price and lose sales. Here's the mistake:

They say to the walk-in, *"How may I help you?"* or *"What kind of flooring do you have in mind?"*

Several bad things happen when a salesperson does this.

**First, it creates no differentiation.** If the prospect has visited other flooring stores, she has already heard this exact same opening line from the other stores' sales people. So, you've created zero differentiation. You only have one chance to make a first impression, and an opener like this gives prospects the impression that you are exactly like everyone else.

**Second, it gives the prospect control of the sales process.** If you don't have a system for selling, you'll always be at the mercy of your prospect's system for buying. Therefore, it's critical that you take control of the sales process within the first 30 seconds of interaction with the prospect.

But when you ask, "How may I help you?" or "What kind of flooring did you have in mind?" this puts the prospect firmly in the driver's seat. The prospect replies, "I'm looking for laminate for my kitchen." The salesperson then schleps the prospect over to the laminate display. And what's the first question out of the prospect's mouth? "How much is this?" The prospect is now running the show. This also leads to the next problem.

**Third, it introduces a premature price discussion.** When a prospect asks about price, most of the time it's because she simply doesn't know enough about flooring to ask educated questions, so she asks the first thing that pops into her head: *What's the price?* But the salesperson is already feeling stressed at having to deal with yet another "price shopper," and is mentally lowering the margins.

Price should never, ever, ever, ever come up until the end of the sales process, and it should always come up at the exact time of your choosing. It should only happen after your prospect has gone through the entire sales process and has seen testimonials, guarantees, and warranties, been thoroughly wowed, and understands that you are utterly, totally, and completely different from all other dealers. Then when you present a price with 45%-50% margins, she'll be much less price resistant. She'll understand why she should pay more. She'll "get it."

## The Pattern Interrupt

So when a prospect comes into your store, instead of saying, "How may I help you?" or "What kind of flooring did you have in mind?" do something completely unexpected. I teach my dealers to say, "Welcome to Jimbo's Floors! Are you a new or returning customer? A new customer! Excellent! We have a special program for new customers. Can I take a quick minute and tell you about it?" If she is a returning customer say, "Excellent! We have a special program for returning customers. Can I take a quick minute and tell you about it?" The "program" is the step-by-step *Design Audit.* Done correctly, most walk-ins will say "yes." This gives the salesperson instant control of the process and creates total differentiation.

This also acts as a pattern interrupt. The prospect walks into your store with her own agenda and expectations. She expects you to say the exact same thing she's heard at every other flooring store she's visited. Following this strategy interrupts this pattern, forces her to pause, and gives you the chance to take total control of the sales process.

## Step 2: Build Value in the Process

When a prospect agrees to hear about your "special program," you now have about 30 seconds to "sell" her on sitting down with you. For example, explain how there are thousands of flooring products, and your process will help narrow it down to the best product for her unique situation and lifestyle.

## Step 3: Ask Questions to Close More Sales

When you visit your doctor, does he burst into the exam room and say, "Hey, we've got a 2-for-1 special on Viagra! Also, 50% off penicillin! And this week we're having our antidepressant blowout sale! Save up to 70% on Lexapro, Zoloft, and Prozac!"

No, those are used car salesman tactics. Instead, he sits down with you, asks you questions, and writes down the answers in your chart. He finds out what's ailin' ya, and then (and only then) does he prescribe a course of treatment.

You want to position yourself as a Trusted Advisor, like the family doctor. Not like a used car salesman. An effective way to create the Trusted Advisor positioning is to ask lots of questions. So, sit down with your prospect and ask questions about her lifestyle, level of traffic, the kind of flooring she currently owns, how she has maintained it, etc. Write down the answers.

## Step 4: Wow the Customer During the In-Home Visit

Most dealers simply show up, take measurements, leave, and then email or call the prospect with a price. This is an enormous missed opportunity to wow the prospect, create differentiation, and position yourself as a Trusted Advisor.

 When the salesperson visits a prospect's home to measure, he should be trained not only to get measurements, but also to inspect the customer's vacuum, the walk-off mats, the kind of carpet spotter she is using, etc. He should also give written recommendations on floor maintenance.

Your entire process should be written out, including sales scripts for each stage of the process.

Finally, a word of warning: This process has been proven to work in my own business, and by the many dealers I've trained to do it. But occasionally a dealer will tell me that many of their walk-ins won't go through the process. Invariably, upon further questioning, I find out that the dealer is not using sales scripts, or in some other way is messing up the process. So, if you get pushback from a high percentage of walk-ins, don't assume they are all price shoppers. And don't give up on this system: It works. Look at what you and your team may be doing inadvertently to sabotage your results.

## CASE STUDY

## How a New-to-the-Industry Salesperson Increased His Closed Sale Ratio to 85% With High Margins

A big challenge for dealers is finding sales people with experience in the flooring industry. If none are to be found, dealers must hire people without experience, which means many months of training before they become producers for the business. And after all that work? Often the salesperson will quit, or go to work for a competitor. But what if there's a better way? What if you could get a total newbie salesperson producing big revenue for your business in just weeks instead of months?

 That's exactly what happens for dealers who use the *Design Audit™*. Daniel (photo, right) is a salesperson for Russ (left), a dealer from Utah. Daniel had very little experience in the flooring business when he began using the *Design Audit*. Here's what Daniel told me:

"I started only six months ago in the flooring business. I'm very green. Before using the *Design Audit*, my residential margins were 30%-35%. It was emotionally stressful. I'd end the day, be totally exhausted, and realize I hadn't closed any sales. It was discouraging. We're right down the street from two home stores. People would come in and say, 'Lowe's quoted me this price,' or 'Home Depot quoted me such and such.' I was constantly having to compete on price. I started using the *Design Audit* just a couple of months ago. I closed the first seven out of seven people that I used the *Design Audit* on. Since then, my overall close ratio has averaged 85%. Our residential margins are now averaging 40%."

I asked Russ how it feels having a system that you can turn over to a totally new, green, never-worked-in-the-flooring-business-before salesperson, and have him instantly begin generating these kinds of margins and close ratios. Here's what he said:

"It's pretty amazing, and gives me a lot of hope about building my business. In the past I felt like it's really hard to bring someone new in. It takes a couple of years to get them trained. What if during that time they aren't successful, and they don't generate enough money, and you have to start over from scratch? So to be able to put somebody into a system takes a lot of pressure off of me from needing to teach them everything about how to close a sale. The tools are there for them to be able to do that with the *Design Audit*. Hiring a new salesperson is always kind of scary; it's kind of a crapshoot. I think other dealers can relate to this. You can bring in a good person but put them into a bad sales system, and they may not last very long. But you can bring a mediocre person in and put them in the right system, and even they can be successful. We're also getting higher margins by using the *Design Audit*. So even though we cut all our advertising, our net profits have literally tripled."

## RUN THE NUMBERS

 If your sales team is trained on the *Design Audit* system, each team member should be able to close at least one extra sale per week. Dealers using the *Design Audit* say this is conservative, but let's go with that number.

Average ticket: $3,000

3 sales people x 1 extra sale per week = $9,000

$9,000 x 52 weeks = $468,000

That's nearly half a million dollars in additional revenue with ZERO marketing costs.

CHAPTER 6

# AFTER: HOW TO DOUBLE THE VALUE OF EVERY CUSTOMER

Now we're going to dive deep into the two strategies in the *After* step. These are what you do after the sale to generate repeat and referral business, fence your herd in, and keep poachers out.

One of the biggest mistakes we see is that the vast majority of dealers totally ignore their past customers because they have the hunter mentality. They're so busy going from job to job that they don't do any follow-up. It's a series of one-night stands with no relationship. Most flooring dealers get as much repeat business from their customers as funeral home directors.

Have you ever gone in to install carpets, discovered that your customer had someone else install wood, and then he says to you, "Oh wow, I didn't know you did that, too!" An *After* system makes sure this never happens.

The *After* step is critical because box stores are lurking in every city and everywhere online, spending millions of dollars in advertising to poach your customers from you. Every rancher worth his rations has a way to keep poachers out, and predators from getting to his herd. There's a posse of apron-wearing desperados backed up by millions of dollars in TV advertising coming for your customers. Are you going to surrender? Are you going to let them poach your customers? I ain't afraid of no apron-wearing hipster with false promises of free installation. You won't be either when you have the *After* step working for you.

## After Strategy #1: The *Neighborhood Advisor*

The *Neighborhood Advisor* works by using a strategic outreach and messaging process that gets you repeat business from customers, and referrals to their friends and family, and lets you sell to them in a competition-free zone.

We use two primary tools for accomplishing this: *The Neighborhood Advisor* printed newsletter, which goes out monthly to our dealers' past customers, and The *Neighborhood Advisor* email newsletter, which goes out weekly. Some dealers have asked me, "Wow, Jim, isn't that much communication going to annoy people?" Well, if you do like most dealers and send out nothing but flooring advertisements, then yes, people will opt out of your emails and throw out your mailers.

But we have developed a unique messaging formula that enables you to stay in front of your customers week in and week out, and have them look forward to hearing from you. In fact, this formula is so powerful that we regularly hear comments like this one from Dan, a dealer in Montana:

## CASE STUDY
### Dan Quit All "Traditional" Advertising Cold Turkey, His Margins Are at 45% or More, and His Store Is Thriving!

Dan Ginnaty is a dealer from Montana. Like many dealers, he got an early start in flooring. His dad was an installer, so he's been around the business since he was 5 years old.

Dan cancelled almost all of his traditional advertising (going "cold turkey," as he put it) and replaced it with *The Neighborhood Advisor.*

**His customers call when they move to provide their new address so they can receive his newsletter at their new home.** I asked Dan if he ever got this response from customers with traditional advertising. "Never happened," he said.

Which makes sense. Think back to the last time you moved. Did you call all the companies sending you advertisements and give them your forwarding address? Of course not. But dealers sending a direct-response newsletter get those calls regularly. This is because this type of newsletter is more like getting a magazine than an advertisement.

Not only is Dan getting customers through the newsletter, but the type of customer is different. "We're talking to people on a monthly basis minimum who have proven that they will give us their money in the past, and the likelihood that they'll do so in the future is greatly improved over someone listening to the radio or seeing you on TV." Dan has seen that the way they are perceived and received by the consumer is different: "They're almost friends when they come in. They know what we look like because we have our picture in the newsletter … it's very friendly."

And unlike most "traditional" flooring ads, Dan's newsletter doesn't rely on "cheap-price" offers to get people in the door. "My residential margins are at 45%," Dan told me recently. "And I just did a $120,000 commercial job with 50% margins."

Think about that for a minute. The last time you moved, did you call the companies sending you junk mail and give them your forwarding address? No way! In fact, people sort their mail over a trash can, throwing away anything that looks like an advertisement. And that's what happens with most mailers and emails sent out by dealers. But what if you could send out messages that follow a proven formula that make your customers look forward to hearing from you, and even give you their forwarding address when they move, like they do for Dan and other dealers using the Flooring Success System? You can, and it's called the 90/10 formula.

## The 90/10 Formula

This means sending content that's 90% fun, informative, welcome, entertaining, educational communication, and only 10% about flooring. Remember … all flooring all the time is boring. The average person just isn't into an announcement about the newest laminate.

Also, each issue of *The Neighborhood Advisor* contains nine emotional triggers that make people want to open it, read it, and respond to it. Here are two triggers you can start using today in your messages to past customers:

51

**The first emotional trigger is customer recognition.** People love to see their names in print or in emails, and they love to be recognized. So, feature a "customer of the month." People are also curious and want to see who your "customer of the month" is, so they'll open your newsletter or email to find out. This creates strong connections with your herd of customers, develops a sense of community, and demonstrates over and over again that you care about them and appreciate their business.

**The second emotional trigger is having a customer involvement device.** This gets people actively involved with your business every month, and makes them want to open and read your newsletter. An effective involvement device we use in every issue is a monthly trivia contest. It features a trivia question, and invites readers to email in their answer. Everyone with the correct answer is entered into a drawing for a gift card for dinner or movie tickets. It also congratulates the winner of the previous month's contest.

Some dealers in my exclusive marketing program have doubled and even tripled their revenue by implementing *The Neighborhood Advisor* newsletter and email strategy. This gets you off the boom and bust roller coaster and replaces it with the peace of mind of a steady stream of honest customers year-round. It's even saved dealers who were on the verge of closing their doors. Dealers like Mark.

## CASE STUDY

## Illinois Dealer Was On The Verge Of Closing His Doors

Mark Bouquet is a dealer from Illinois. He had been in business for 19 years when the recession and housing crash happened in 2008. At that time, 80% of his business was new construction.

To make matters much worse, his county put a moratorium on new building permits. Because 80% of his business was new construction, he was on the verge of closing his doors and seeing 20 years of hard work go down the drain. The stress and heartache were almost unimaginable. It was a terrible, frightening time for him and his family. That's when he reached out to me, and began using *The Neighborhood Advisor* newsletter strategy. Fast forward six months. Mark was now booked out solid for four to six weeks, with more business than he could handle. His business was now 90% residential remodel. By marketing to his past customers, he was able to rapidly transition from a new construction business to a residential remodel business. Recently Mark did over $4 million in revenue. Here's a note he sent me:

"Jim ... our business is growing exponentially. There is no comparison between my company now and before I joined Flooring Success Systems. I can't believe the turnaround here! October was our busiest month in 20 years. November was our second busiest month. And this month we are crashing new records! I truly believe you were a Godsend. Thank you!"
*– Mark Bouquet, Illinois*

## RUN THE NUMBERS

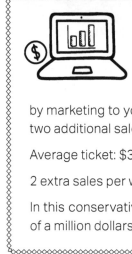

Every floor dealership is sitting on an untapped gold mine: their past customer list. I've seen dealers totally transform their business by using *The Neighborhood Advisor* to mine the gold. Let's be ultraconservative and say that by marketing to your list of past customers you only generate two additional sales per week.

Average ticket: $3,000

2 extra sales per week x 52 weeks = $312,000

In this conservative scenario, you're generating an extra third of a million dollars. I've seen dealers do much more than this.

## After Strategy #2: Referral Connections
## 5 Reasons You Need More Referrals

1. Customers who are referred to you are already "pre-sold" on your service.
2. You get the "halo" effect. Happy customers who refer you to a friend or relative are giving you a halo of credibility.
3. Referrals are less skeptical. After all, if someone's brother-in-law, or aunt, or best friend referred you, you must be pretty damn fantastic!
4. Referrals have lower price resistance than cold prospects.
5. Referrals have extremely low marketing costs.

In spite of these benefits, only a tiny fraction of dealers have a system in place to maximize their referrals. For most dealers, referrals are a "happy accident." They do a decent job, and eventually they get some referrals. But there is no system in place to generate a steady stream of ongoing referrals.

**What The...?!**

# Most Dealers Don't Have a Referral Generating System in Place

Imagine the owner of a multimillion-dollar home. She wants hardwood installed throughout. This is easily a $50,000+ job. Where do you think this customer is going to look for a flooring dealer? Online? On the radio? Billboards?

Fat chance.

She is going to ask people in her own sphere—other million-dollar homeowners—who they bought their floors from.

The dealers I coach routinely get their largest sales from referrals. Here are just a few examples:

- Mark from Illinois landed a multistate, high-six-figure commercial account from a referral.

- Dan from Montana got his first $100,000 commercial account from a referral. He got a 50% margin on this sale, virtually unheard of for a commercial job, especially one this size.

- Brent from Utah got a $40,000 residential job from a referral from a Realtor.

- Jimmy from North Carolina regularly sells $10,000, $20,000, $30,000+ residential jobs, and virtually all of them come from referrals.

- Jerome from Texas routinely does residential sales in excess of $10,000, most from referrals.

Think back to your 10 largest sales of the past year. I'll bet you the biggest pizza in Chicago that most of them came from repeat/referral customers.

## 5-Step Referral Marketing System

Referrals are so valuable that you should not passively wait for your customers to send you referrals. But that's exactly what most floor dealers do. At best, referrals are a "welcome surprise." By having a referral marketing system in place, you can dramatically increase the number of referrals you get.

In just a minute I'll give you the steps to the *Referral Connections™* system that members of our Flooring Success Systems program are taught, but first things first …

## Be Referable

Being referable is the first and most critical step to getting referrals. I know it sounds obvious, but a lot of dealers neglect this, so it needs to be said. You've got to provide great service and great products if you want referrals.

Great service begins with the basics, what I call "blocking and tackling."

- Return phone calls promptly.
- Show up on time.
- Call your customers five minutes before you arrive at their home.
- Dress professionally.
- Say "please" and "thank you."
- Be courteous and polite.
- Honor your warranties and guarantees.
- Under promise, over deliver.
- Be honest, especially if you have to give your customer bad news, like that special order of hardwood got delayed because of a blizzard.
- Do what you say you're going to do, when you say you're going to do it.

If you're unwilling to do these basic things, you'll always struggle to get referrals. Don't ignore the basics. Now on to the 5-step *Referral Connections system.*

## Step 1: Schedule a Follow-Up Visit

Meet with your customer after the installation is complete. This can be done in her home or in the store. Use the following script:

*"Mrs. Jones, now it's time to schedule your post-installation follow-up visit. John will do a walkthrough with you and inspect the installation to make sure everything is perfect. Are mornings or afternoons better for you?"*

Notice that I don't say, "Can we meet?" That gives her a yes or no option. Instead, I give her two yes options: morning or afternoon. I also treat the follow-up visit as standard and customary; it's part of the usual process, just like scheduling the installation.

If you can't get to the customer's home, schedule an appointment for her to come into your store to meet with the salesperson. Tell her that you've got a thank you gift for her.

## Step 2: Wow the Customer

Arrive on time. Call a few minutes before you arrive for your appointment.

- Bring a surprise gift for the customer.
- Wear protective shoe covers.
- Once inside, do a walkthrough and make sure the installation looks good. Tell her how great the new floors look, and reinforce to the customer what a great choice she made.

## Step 3: Request Referrals

Most dealers never ask for referrals. At best they use an "oh, by the way approach" and say something like, "I'm glad you are happy with your new floors, Mrs. Gopherhoser. We'd really appreciate it if you passed our name along to anyone you know who needs flooring." This is not going to generate many referrals beyond what you are already getting.

The dealers in our program are taught an "on-purpose" referral request strategy. First, they transition from talking about the customer's floors to educating her on their referral program. This transition is carefully scripted: "Mrs. Smith, now I'd like to take a minute and tell you about our referral program."

Next, they use an actual referral form. This form explains how she and her friends will benefit from the referral program. Some important points on the form include:

- **Advertising is very expensive, so rather than pay the TV or radio station, you'd rather reward your customers.**
- **She'll be doing her friends a HUGE favor by referring a company they can trust.**
- **Each of her referrals will get a gift certificate to your store in her name.**

If you can't possibly meet with the customer in her home, then let her know you've got a thank you gift waiting at your store, and schedule an appointment for her to meet with her salesperson. Present her with your referral program and referral form while she's in your store.

**Watch Out!**

## Don't Expect Customers to Mail In Referral Forms

Leaving a referral form or card behind and hoping the customer will mail it in doesn't work very well. You'll be waiting for the next ice age. In order for this strategy to be fully effective, you should meet with your customer in person, either in her home or in your store.

## Step 4: Automate Your Referral Marketing

We handle the follow-up marketing for our members. Here's how our system works so you can implement it in your own business.

Flooring Success Systems member Bob just completed an installation for Cathy Consumer, and she's thrilled with her new floors. When he arrives to do a walk-through of her home, he presents her with a nice gift bag. After the walkthrough he takes her through the referral request form and explains all the benefits of the Referral Connections program. Cathy fills out the form and gives him five names. When Bob gets back to the office he (or his assistant) goes online and enters the names into his custom online referral form. Our team takes over from there. We send all five of the referrals a letter introducing each of them to Bob's business. Included in the letter is a gift certificate to Bob's Floors from Cathy Consumer.

## Step 5: Follow Up With Referrals

Some of the referrals will purchase flooring immediately, but some won't be in the market right then. So they are subscribed to *The Neighborhood Advisor* newsletter. Why? Because they are incredibly valuable leads. They've been referred to Bob's business by someone they know. They got a letter from Bob introducing himself. Enclosed in the letter was a gift certificate from their friend, Cathy Consumer. This is an extremely effective introduction to Bob's business.

My team subscribes all the referrals—even those who didn't buy immediately—to *The Neighborhood Advisor.* Each month the referrals get a newsletter that's fun, entertaining, informative, and educational. Who do you think is going to be at the top of the list when they are finally ready to purchase floors? Bob! Many times the dealers in my program and I have had referrals—who haven't even purchased yet—send us additional referrals because they are so impressed with the follow-up.

## How David Made an Extra $90,463 in One Month

Having a Referral Marketing System in place can produce big revenue gains in a short time, like it did for David Kocian, a dealer from Texas.

After he joined Flooring Success Systems, he began to implement the *Referral Connections*™ system. The results were amazing. "I made an extra $90,463 in one month! During a slow economy!" he told me.

 "My sales people had huge grins on their faces as they turned in their paperwork each week," he said. "They were thrilled at how much revenue we were generating with just one simple strategy. It's hard to describe how good that felt!"

Roughly half of the $90k came from a single job, which isn't surprising. Think back to your last 10 large jobs; chances are that most of them were repeat or referral customers. This is because when people are going to buy tens-of-thousands of dollars in flooring, they usually get referrals. There's too much money at stake to risk hiring someone off a website or a radio ad.

By having the Referral Connections in place, you will not only increase the number of average-sized sales, but you'll put yourself in a position to land more of the larger jobs that usually can't be had through traditional advertising.

## RUN THE NUMBERS

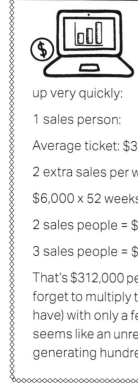

If your team was trained on the *Referral Connections* system, each salesperson could conservatively get an extra couple of referral sales per week. The revenue adds up very quickly:

1 sales person:

Average ticket: $3,000

2 extra sales per week = $6,000

$6,000 x 52 weeks = $312,000

2 sales people = $624,000

3 sales people = $936,000

That's $312,000 per year in extra revenue per salesperson (don't forget to multiply this figure by the number of sales people you have) with only a few hundred dollars in marketing costs. If this seems like an unrealistic number to you, cut it in half. You're still generating hundreds of thousands of dollars in extra revenue.

CHAPTER 7

# HOW DEALERS ARE GETTING 70% CLOSE RATIOS

You've met dealers in this book with close rates double that of the industry average. However, I've had skeptics say, *"Jim, when someone says they're closing 70% of their sales, I don't believe them because the national average is 32%."* Let's get something straight—I have no interest in helping dealers to be "average." I want you to blow the doors off industry averages. I want you to dominate your market and beat the boxes, just like the dealers in this book are doing.

It's important to remember that effective marketing is a function of sifting, sorting, and screening, bringing in the gold nuggets—qualified buyers who are ready, willing, and able to buy right now, even if you're more expensive. Effective marketing sifts out most of the price shoppers and time wasters. The *Before, During, and After* system is a highly effective sifting, sorting, and screening machine.

Some dealers pump out hundreds-of-thousands of dollars in advertising to drive traffic to their store. Some have invested a fortune to locate their store in a high-traffic area, which generates a lot of walk-ins. When you're driving a large volume of cold traffic to your store in this way, you're going to have lower close rates. It's because you're attracting a high percentage of unqualified prospects, meaning prospects who have not been sifted, sorted, and screened, and who are not ready, willing, and able to buy right now. This method can work, but there's a lot of wasted money. There's also a lot of wasted time because, instead of your marketing doing the sifting, sorting, and screening, and bringing you gold nuggets, your sales people wind up doing it manually. That's what happened to this dealer:

## CASE STUDY
## Too Much Of The Wrong Kind Of Walk-In Traffic Is Hurting This Dealer

I know a dealer from Florida whose store is located next to a busy freeway. His signage is clearly visible to thousands of drivers who pass by every day. He has a ton of walk-in traffic, but his close ratio is only about 15%. He's pulling his hair out because his sales people are wasting a staggering amount of time with people who never buy. His biggest problem is that far too many unqualified people are coming into his store. He has no sifting and sorting mechanism in place, so the high volume of traffic is an impediment, not a help.

With that said, how can the average dealer achieve close ratios of 70% or more? By implementing the entire *Before, During, and After* system, including the *Design Audit*. Let's break down how the entire system works together to increase your closed sale ratio.

## Before

You've got the review system in place, so you're generating an ongoing stream of positive reviews online. Long before Cathy Consumer ever sets foot in your store, she has seen your reviews, and this positions you as totally different from your competitors (sifting, sorting, and screening).

Cathy opted in for the Consumer's Guide to Floor Covering when she visited your website. (You also hand out printed copies to every walk-in.) The guide positions you as a Trusted Advisor, and answers the unspoken question: *Why should I choose you instead of your competitors?*

Because she opted in for the guide, Cathy was also plugged into the follow-up email campaign. Before she ever visits your store, she's been getting an email every few days further positioning you and your team as a trusted authority, and further answering the unspoken question. Every email has customer testimonials, which are powerful social proof, just like reviews (more sifting, sorting, and screening).

When she finally visits your store, Cathy walks in with a very different impression of you than any other dealer. Remember Matt Capell from a previous chapter? He has more than 120 reviews, and his customers regularly tell him that 1) they visited his store because of his reviews, and 2) his prices are higher than his competition, but they're going to buy from him anyway because of his reviews. His marketing has sifted, sorted, and screened out the price shoppers, and brings him the gold nuggets. The same can happen for you.

## During

The *Design Audit* process continues the work that began in the *Before* step: *answering the unspoken question.* It takes Cathy through a carefully choreographed, step-by-step experience that's unlike anything she would experience with another dealer. The process has 21 trust-builders built into it, which position your sales team as Trusted Advisors. It creates total, utter, complete differentiation from any of your competitors—apples and oranges. It gives you the power to get higher margins, and generate higher average tickets, and—this is key—*increase your closed sale ratio.*

## After

Your team has been trained on how to use the Referral Connections system to generate referrals from your completed installations, including Cathy's. Each member of your team is now getting more referrals than ever before.

Cathy and the rest of your customer list are subscribed to *The Neighborhood Advisor* past customer marketing system. They hear from you regularly with communication using the 90/10 formula: 90% welcome, fun, informative, entertaining communication, which includes nine emotional triggers that make people look forward to hearing from you, open your newsletters (printed and email), read them, and respond.

Maybe right now 25% of your walk-ins are repeat or referred customers. But over time the strategies in the After step will cause that percentage to increase to 50% or more. Repeat and referred clients already know you, like you, and trust you. So, when you generate more repeat and referral business, your closed sale ratio automatically goes up. Some dealers I work with generate over 80% of their revenue from repeat and referral customers. Their close ratios are through the roof.

Each step of the *Before, During, and After* system by itself is powerful, but when they're working together, the results can be jaw-dropping because each step reinforces the other steps. Each step working together is what generates close ratios of 50%-70% or more. The whole is more effective than the sum of its parts. If you want to transform your closed sale ratios while getting high margins, you need to have the entire *Before, During, and After* system in place.

CHAPTER 8

# HOW TO SET UP YOUR *IDEAL BUSINESS* SO YOU CAN LIVE AN *IDEAL LIFESTYLE*

### Why Making More Money Is Only a First Step

Making lots of money is a prerequisite to having the life you want. After all, if you're broke and barely keeping your doors open, you won't have the money to pay for three weeks vacation in the Caribbean. That's why the subtitle of this book is *make more, work less, and get your life back.* The "make more" part is critical. But it's not enough. In fact, I've met a lot of dealers who were making plenty of money, but were still trapped working way too many hours. Dealers like Derek ...

**CASE STUDY**

**This Dealer Was A Successful Slave**

Derek is a dealer from North Carolina who came to me for help with his business. He was making a personal salary of $400,000 from his dealership, but he was working 60-plus hours per week including weekends. He took very little time off, and didn't get to spend nearly as much time with his daughters as he wanted. He was a typical "successful slave." After a couple of months of coaching him, he freed up an entire day per week without adding any more staffing. He sent me an email not long after that telling me about taking his daughters on a vacation to Disney World.

This situation is not uncommon. I've lost count of the number of dealers who have come to me who had multimillion-dollar businesses, but were completely enslaved, stressed out, and miserable. This is because once you're making plenty of money, you'll still remain enslaved to your business if you don't have systems in place to unshackle you.

My goal is to open your eyes to a new way of looking at your business. This new perspective is key to finally taking control of your time and your life. Let's jump in.

## What Is the Primary Purpose of Your Flooring Business?

I'll answer this by first telling you what the primary purpose of your flooring business is not. The primary purpose of your flooring business is not to ...

1. Provide employment
2. Help customers

3. Pay taxes
4. Support charitable causes
5. Sell flooring

I know that may shock you, especially the last one. But I firmly believe that none of these is the primary purpose of your flooring business. Yes, they are important things. Some are even vital to the success of your business and, in the case of #3, to staying out of jail! But NONE of these is the *primary* purpose of your business.

**The primary purpose of your business is this:** *to fund and facilitate your ideal lifestyle.*

If your business is not providing you with plenty of time and freedom to enjoy life, then what is the point of putting in all the hard work and taking the risks of being an entrepreneur? If you're providing employment, helping customers, and all those other things, what good does it do you personally if you feel stuck, working 50 to 70 hours per week, stressed out, never taking vacations, and wishing for something better?

## Why You Started Your Own Flooring Dealership

In reality, when you started your flooring business or took over an existing one, you probably did it because you wanted a better life for yourself and your family. And you believed that owning your own flooring business was the best route for making that happen. After all, you could have gotten a traditional job working for someone else.

So, what are the dreams that motivated you to own a flooring dealership? I don't mean simply to "make more money." I mean what do you dream about when you're all alone driving to measure a home or when you're lying awake at night? What are the things you desperately wish you could do that you're not? Maybe they're things that you keep to yourself, that you don't tell anyone because you think they might sound silly. Maybe you don't talk about your dreams because you've given up hope of ever achieving them. It hurts too damn much to talk about. If that describes you, believe me, I get it. I've been there. And I've found my way out of that miserable situation. And I've helped other dealers find their way out. Stick with me, because I can help you, too. I mean it.

Or maybe you're not feeling quite that desperate. Maybe you simply want more out of your business and your life, and you're feeling stuck, not knowing exactly how to get there. I've helped many dealers in your situation get "un-stuck" and achieve a whole new level in their flooring business and personal life. I've got you covered, too.

So, I want you to take a minute and write down ONE thing you dream about having in your life that you don't have right now because of a lack of time, money, or both. Don't worry about it sounding impossible right now, just write it down. And be honest. It's your life after all.

I'll wait.

*****

Welcome back. Did you write down your ONE big dream? Or are you having trouble coming up with anything? If so, that's okay. It may have been so long since you've dreamed about the life you really want that you find it hard to articulate. Maybe your dream is buried deep. But I know it's there, way down inside.

Here are some ideas to get the wheels turning:

- "I only work Monday through Thursday, and I quit early on Wednesdays. Wednesday afternoons and all day Friday I play golf."
- "I take three multi-week vacations every year, many out of the country. While I'm gone, my business runs without me. I never call the office when I'm on vacation. There's never a pile of catch-up work when I get back."
- "I take a nap every afternoon."
- "I start work at 10:00 each morning. I spend the early mornings hanging out with my spouse."
- "I quit each day by 3:00 p.m. so I can coach my kid's soccer team."

- "I built a cabin in the woods to spend time with my family, especially my dad, who had a terminal illness. My dad and I spent a lot of time there together before he passed away. Having the time to spend at that cabin with him ... priceless. I wouldn't trade it for anything."
- "Every day I get to the store at 10:00 a.m. and leave by 5:00 p.m. I take every Friday, Saturday, and Sunday off. Every week I get a three-day weekend!"
- "I finally got my pilot's license."
- "My wife and I are building our dream home."

By the way ... every dream on that list came from a floor dealer I worked with. Every single one of them was achieved in spite of many of the dealers having given up on those dreams before coming to me. Some of them were achieved in a breathtakingly short period of time. If they can do it, so can you. You just need the right blueprint.

## The *Ideal Business, Ideal Lifestyle* Blueprint

Imagine a man who wants to build a house. He has a vague idea in his mind of what he wants it to look like. So, he orders a bunch of lumber, and once it arrives he starts driving nails through boards, hoping that when they are all nailed together he'll have a house. When it's finished, he's disappointed. After all that hard work, his new house is lopsided, the doors don't close right, it's drafty in the wind, and it's leaky in the rain.

No one in their right mind would build a house that way. The first thing you'd do is draw up a set of blueprints on paper. This way you can design your house exactly the way you want it. If you change your mind on where to put a bedroom or the kitchen, it's easy to make those changes. Only when you have your house drawn out exactly the way you want it on the blueprint would you start building.

Unfortunately, most dealers start their flooring business without a blueprint. They have a rough idea of what they want it to look like. They know they want to have a store (or a mobile showroom) that sells flooring, and they want to make money. But beyond that, it's all pretty vague. Once the business is built, they become frustrated because they are working

60-plus hours per week, feeling stressed, and hitting a glass ceiling that keeps them from growing any bigger. They find themselves slaves to the business they created. All of this could have been avoided if they'd started with a blueprint of an *Ideal Business* that funded and facilitated their *Ideal Lifestyle.*

The good news is that even though you may have built your business without a blueprint, you can go back and remodel it. Transform it, actually. I've helped many dealers transform their businesses into *ideal* businesses so they can live their *ideal* lifestyles. Here's an overview of the process I take dealers through to help them make this transformation.

## Step 1: Design Your *Ideal Lifestyle*

When dealers start a business (or take over an existing one), often they are so focused on growing revenue, hiring, and wearing 20 different hats that their business takes over their life. They spend less and less time doing what has meaning, purpose, and value to them outside of work. They reach a point where they are trying to fit their life into the tiny cracks of time that are left over at the end of a 60-hour week. This is completely backward.

Instead, I coach dealers on how to create a blueprint of the exact lifestyle they want. Then and only then do I have them create a blueprint of a business that will fund and facilitate that lifestyle. You want to build your business around your life. You want your business to fund and facilitate your *Ideal Lifestyle.*

If you've spent years burning the candle at both ends in order to operate your business, this may sound like a crazy pipe dream. But I've helped many dealers who were stressed out, burned out, and enslaved to totally reengineer their businesses and finally achieve the dreams that inspired them to go into business for themselves in the first place. Some are taking multiple vacations every year and working less than 35 hours per week (no weekends), with plenty of freedom to pursue hobbies, time with family, physical fitness, fishing, you name it.

The first step in achieving your *Ideal Business* and *Ideal Lifestyle* is to get a very clear picture of what you want your life to look like. Here's a sampling of some of the questions I walk dealers through to help them create a picture of the life they want.

**Describe how you take care of your body, your health, and your well-being.**

How many times a week do you walk or jog? How often do you get a massage? What kinds of food do you eat? What is your level of fitness? Do you study martial arts? Do you weight-lift? How often do you get out into nature for walks in the woods or along the beach and get fresh air?

**Describe your home.**

Where do you live geographically? What does your house look like? How many square feet? How many bedrooms? How large is your property? Is it in the country? Urban? Suburban? Do you have a pond? Do you live by a creek? Is your home well organized? What does your bedroom look like? Do you have a den or a library or other personal space? What does your personal space look like?

**What do you do for enjoyment and recreation?**

You have freedom, so what do you fill your free time? Hobbies? Writing? Fishing? Bicycling? Backpacking? Cooking? Hosting gourmet dinner parties with friends and family? Road trips? Driving from Maine to California and staying in bed and breakfasts along the way? BBQs by the pool with all your neighbors?

**Are you involved in volunteer work?**

Coaching your kid's sports team? Teaching kids how to fish? Teaching an adult literacy class? Fund-raising for a women's shelter? Beginning a trust fund for a favorite charity?

**What are your big, unusual, or "crazy" dreams?**

These are the things that cause you to say: Wouldn't it be neat to ... Take a month in the Caribbean? Hike in the Himalayas? Take up rock climbing? Go surfing in Hawaii? Hike the Pacific Crest Trail? Fly-fish for tarpon in Florida? Go skydiving? Spend a summer touring Europe? Live in Spain for a month? Bike ride from Canada to Mexico to raise money for Feed the Children? Take culinary classes? Get your pilot's license? Walk across the state to raise money for my favorite charity?

**Describe what your perfect week looks like.**

What time do you get up each morning on weekdays? Weekends?

Do you take your kids to school? Pick them up? Coach their little league team? Volunteer at your child's school?

Do you have lunch every day at your favorite restaurant with a different friend? Do you go fly-fishing every Wednesday afternoon? Golf every Thursday? Take a painting class on Tuesday evening? Band rehearsal on Wednesday evenings?

Do you spend each morning from 8:00 to 10:00 practicing martial arts? Exercising? Relaxing with your spouse? Bike riding? Perfecting your golf game? Writing a novel? Training for a marathon?

How many hours per week do you spend working in and on your business? Eight hours per day? Six hours per day? Four days per week, Monday through Thursday? Do you show up at 10:00 a.m., quit at 3:00 p.m.?

Most people have never thought about or created a picture of their life in this way. It's a process. Sometimes I'll spend several meetings helping dealers get really clear on what they want their life to look like. Once that's done, we move on to Step 2.

## Step 2: Design Your *Ideal Business*

Next, I have dealers create a blueprint of their *Ideal Business*. Here's a sampling of some of the questions I walk them through to create their blueprint:

**Describe your ideal work week.**

How many days per month do you spend at your business? Which days? On the days you are at the store, what time do you arrive? What time do you leave?

**Exactly what tasks do you do during those hours?**

Think in terms of working on your business. Developing and implementing sales and marketing strategies. Strategic planning. Developing affiliate relationships. Implementing systems.

**How much does your business do in gross sales each year?**

Be specific.

**What's your personal net income each year (pre-taxes)?**

Be specific.

**How many store locations do you have?**

**What does your store look like?**

Where is it located geographically? How many square feet of retail space? How many square feet of warehouse? Is it neat and clean? What does the sign look like? Is your office organized? What do the displays look like? Do you have a mobile showroom instead of a retail store?

**Describe your team.**

*Sales people:* How many sales people? Are they neat, clean, and professional? Do your customers perceive them as Trusted Advisors? Do they look out for the needs of your customers? Are they "closers"—can they follow the *Design Audit* and make the sale? Are they team players? Are they well paid? Low turnover? Happy to be a part of your team? Are they willing to follow the systems that give you "walk-away" power?

*Installers:* Are they on staff, subcontractors, or a combination? Are they neat, clean, and professional? Are they ambassadors, representing your store in a professional manner? Do they "wow" your customers with fabulous service? Can you count on them to do quality work? Are they team players? Are they well paid? Low turnover? Happy to be a part of your team? Are they willing to follow the systems that give you "walk-away" power?

*Support/administrative staff:* Are they neat, clean, and professional? Are they ambassadors, representing your store in a professional manner? Do they "wow" your customers with fabulous service? Can you count on them to do quality work? Are they team players? Are they well paid? Low turnover? Happy to be a part of your team? Are they willing to follow the systems that give you "walk-away" power?

**How does your business function when you're not around?**

Do you have to "check in" with your business all the time, or do you have systems in place so it runs pretty much on its own? Does your staff continue to provide a high level of customer service and satisfaction when you're gone? Do things "fall through the cracks"—get forgotten? Or do your systems allow your business to continue to function like a well-oiled machine? Are you able to stop thinking about your business while you're away?

**Do your customers respect and trust you and your staff?**

**How much of your business comes from repeat and referral customers?**

**Describe any other particulars about your *Ideal Business.***


As they're creating the blueprint, I have them keep the following questions in mind:


- Will the *Ideal Business* I'm describing allow me to live the *Ideal Lifestyle* I described earlier?
- Does it give me enough time to do what has meaning, purpose, and value for me?
- Does it provide the finances I need to pay for my *Ideal Lifestyle*?

## Coaching

It should be obvious that creating a blueprint for your *Ideal Business* and *Ideal Lifestyle* is a process. It takes time to create a plan and then implement that plan so it gives you the results you want. I've found that many dealers benefit by getting help with this process. That's why my company, Flooring Success Systems, not only provides "done-for-you" marketing services, but we couple it with coaching to help dealers work through the *Ideal Business, Ideal Lifestyle* process. We deliver our coaching in a number of ways including live group webinars, video training, and one-on-one sessions. Later in the book I'll give you details on how you can take advantage of this coaching if it's of interest to you.

**CASE STUDY**

## "My Wife and I Went to Cabo ... Our First Vacation in Years!"

"Our big challenge was we were growing quickly with our foot on the gas, but did not have the systems in place to properly take our business to the next level. I was working seven days per week just to keep up. Through Jim's program I've been able to implement systems so I can delegate, and have the peace of mind that things are getting handled correctly without me there to babysit. As a result, I've cut my work hours so I can take weekends off. Also, my wife and I went on vacation to Cabo. It was our first vacation in years. The stress relief is unbelievable."
– Jay Robinson, Virginia

CHAPTER 9

# START YOUR
# TRANSFORMATION TODAY

**The objective is to make more money.** To have a growing, thriving business by attracting the best new customers who are happy to pay full margin because they are buying on service. To increase your closed sales, and to quit wasting time putting together estimates for people who don't buy. To fence in your past customers, to get their next jobs in a competition-free zone, and to get referrals to their friends and family—all while keeping poachers out. To develop a business providing a fantastic income and foundation for personal wealth, with respectful customers, freedom from worry or difficulty in attracting all the good customers you'd like, and the liberty and security to conduct business in a manner that pleases you.

**The objective is to work fewer hours and to get your life back.** To develop a business that works for *you* instead of the other way around. That gives you the freedom to work the hours you want—even if it's only 25 hours per week—to take vacations when you want, and to spend all the time with your family you want. To having a business you look forward to going to, where the environment is stress-free and work is a pleasure. And when you're enjoying yourself away from work, your business continues to run like a well-oiled machine, providing great service to customers and making you lots of money. No babysitting required.

Achieving such objectives is possible. In this book you've already met dealers who have done it. But it is rare. Very rare. I am describing a profoundly different flooring business and life experience. It requires doing just about everything differently. Clues to just how differently have appeared throughout this book.

**First of all,** you've got to dismiss the idea that you can grow your business with the "spray and pray" approach to marketing, spending a fortune on a bunch of different strategies and hoping one of them works. You've got to stop listening to the sales vultures who know nothing about the flooring business, trying to sell you generic SEO, lead generation, social media, pay-per-click, website services, and blah, blah, blah, all with their hefty monthly fees, year-long contracts, and zero accountability. You've got to stop being a "hunter," where you hunt down a customer, bag it, skin it, and then you're off hunting the next one.

Instead, you need to transition to "rancher," where your job is to round up a herd of great customers, fence them in and keep poachers out, and live in style. You do this by implementing the *Before, During, and After* system so you have a reliable way of attracting a herd of the best new customers, closing the sale, and fencing your customers in so you can generate ongoing repeat and referral sales from them. You want to round up a vibrant herd of the best customers who are advocates for your business, and who do the selling for you by sending you referrals to their friends and relatives.

**Second of all,** you've got to stop thinking that your business will someday, somehow magically start working for you, and give you the time and freedom to do the things you want. It won't. You have to have a blueprint to transition from working "in" your business to working "on" your business. To transition from a business you have to babysit to one that runs and makes you money even when you're not around.

If you want the different business-and-life experience that comes from transitioning from hunter to rancher, you need to embrace doing just about everything differently. Differently than your peers and friends in the flooring business. Differently than how you've always done things before. Differently than your prospective customers' worst expectations.

The difference is difference.

My team and I can assist you, if you truly have the courage and drive. If you dare to be different—dare to become great—check out the materials that were included with this book, or visit **FloorDealerSuccess.com** to begin your business-and-life transformation as a member of Flooring Success Systems.

## There are three parts to the Flooring Success Systems program.

**Part 1: "Done-For-You" Marketing.** This is where my team implements all the marketing covered in this book FOR you, delivering you a steady stream of the best customers week-in and week-out, leaving you free to do more important things. We also provide online training for you and your sales team on the *Design Audit*™ selling system and the Referral Connections™ system.

---

**RUN THE NUMBERS**

 Throughout this book I've given you examples of how each marketing strategy, by itself, can add hundreds-of-thousands of dollars to your revenue. Collectively, these strategies can add up to millions of dollars.

---

**Part 2: The *Ideal Business, Ideal Lifestyle* Blueprint**

A proven game plan that dealers across the U.S. and Canada have used to take control of their business and get the fantastic life they deserve. It's a step-by-step process for setting up your business so that it runs without you. You'll gain the freedom to take every Friday off, work less than 35 hours per week, take two months of vacation each year, golf three times per week, spend as much time with your family as you want, or whatever your ideal lifestyle is. This is *the* system for setting up your business so that it works for you instead of the other way around.

**Part 3: Community, Coaching, and Support**

My team and I will come alongside you and hold your hand along each step of your journey toward making more money while working less, achieving the awesome business and lifestyle you deserve. You're not alone anymore.

You'll find details about all three parts of the program in the materials included with this book, or when you visit **FloorDealerSuccess.com.**

Your Partner in Greater Success,

Jim Augustus Armstrong
The "Coach"
President, Flooring Success Systems

## Get started on your journey toward making more money, working fewer hours, and getting your life back today!

Check out the information shipped with this book,
or visit **FloorDealerSuccess.com**

# FLOOR DEALER CASE STUDIES

I began *Flooring Success Systems* in 2007 to help dealers make a lot more money while working a lot less. To help them transform their business into an *Ideal Business* which funds and facilitates their *Ideal Lifestyle*. By implementing the strategies in this book, you can make a lot more money and sell at higher prices. This empowers you to hire strong team members so you can delegate and work less. Instead of spending 60+ hours per week at your business, you can cut that in half and have time for hobbies, golf, fishing, family, or whatever you like. In other words, these strategies can be the doorway to your whole new life in the flooring business.

On the following pages are comments from just some of dealers I've worked with who have transformed their businesses and lives for the better.

## This Utah Dealer Was Skeptical About Flooring Success Systems

Russ Bundy joined Flooring Success Systems right as he made the switch from employee to business owner. Here's how he described his perspective on that decision now:

"When I first decided to join Flooring Success Systems, I definitely had a little bit of hesitation. You wonder, 'Does this really work? Could it really be that different from what everyone else is doing?' And it really is. I think as flooring professionals, we tend to look for customers in all the wrong places. We go after the hardest customer, which doesn't make any sense. Jim teaches you how to go after the customer that's easy to get to, that trusts you already. They're more likely to buy from you, more likely to refer you, and they're easier to work with, too. The biggest thing Jim has done for me was to change my mindset from 'going after every single customer' to 'going after the profitable customers.' It's not about chasing after every possibility at any price point, because you're desperate to get the sale – it's about finding customers who will be good to work with, and who will be a profitable customer over time."

Russ is pretty excited about what he's learned, and the transformational effect this has had on his business. "We are doing amazing thanks in large part to the information I have learned through Flooring Success Systems. I've only owned my flooring business for less than two years now and I just paid it off. The most valuable thing I've learned was surprising to me. You attract a certain kind of fish based on the bait you

II

use. By setting ourselves apart and not making price the bait to attract customers, we've seen a positive change in our clientele and are consistently getting 40%+ margins. Contrast that to the largest dealer in town (doing 3-4 times the amount of business we are) who I've heard through the grapevine is on credit hold with half his suppliers because he's the king of the cheap price rat race."

# How Jerome Raised His Margins From 30% to 50% And Stays Booked Out 6-12 Weeks!

How's business now? Jerome is normally booked out for 2-3 months! He considers it "slow" when he's only booked out for 2 weeks. Why isn't he worried about telling customers they have to wait maybe three months for an installation? Because Jerome has learned to create total differentiation from competitors. Prospects are completely willing to wait weeks or months for their installation, even if a cheaper-priced competitor can do it that day. Most dealers would be terrified to tell a customer they had to wait three months; it's unthinkable. But that's because they have not implemented the strategies Jerome has. He now has total control over his business and his life. He owns his business, not the other way around.

In the meantime, he takes a lot of 3-day weekends and several multi-week vacations every year. While he's gone his business runs like a well-oiled machine because he was able to afford to put a great team in place.

Jerome now owns seven houses (some for rental income) and another on a lake nearby. All but one are paid off, and he owns his store and warehouse free and clear. Before joining *Flooring Success Systems* he only had his own home and one rental property, both with mortgages. By investing the extra profits his business now generates into real estate, Jerome will likely have the option of early retirement if he chooses.

Jerome is proving every day that any floor dealer can build their *Ideal Business* and live their *Ideal Lifestyle*, including you. By implementing the strategies in this book, you can explode your revenue by getting more sales and commanding higher prices. You'll not only be making a lot more money, you'll be

IV

able to afford to hire the best employees so you can delegate and move some of your work off your overloaded plate. Would you like to take 3-day weekends? Take multiple vacations every year? Eliminate the stress? And while you're gone your store continues to run smoothly? Jerome will be the first to tell you that if he can do it, you can, too. Flooring Success Systems is your doorway to a whole new life in the flooring business. To get started today, check out the materials shipped with this book, or visit **FloorDealerSuccess.com.**

## Jimmy Tells Price Shoppers That He's The Most Expensive ... And Still Gets The Sale!

Jimmy Williams is a dealer from North Carolina and has been in business for over 40 years. He has done an outstanding job creating differentiation and positioning himself as a Trusted Advisor. His prices are higher than virtually all his competitors.

Like most dealers, he occasionally has people try to beat him up on price. But he uses one of my sales strategies to instantly turn the tables on them.

"I had a fellow come into the store, trying to beat me up on price," Jimmy told me. "I decided to use the strategy you talk about in your program. I looked him in the eye and told him that we're the highest priced store in the county, and that I'm sorry, but we probably wouldn't be able to help him. I handed him my card, and as I turned away he said, 'But wait ...'"

He bought. At *Jimmy's* price.

This happened twice within a couple of weeks of my conversation with Jimmy. For most dealers, the thought of telling a prospect that they're the most expensive strikes terror in their hearts. But because Jimmy has positioned himself as totally different than competitors, he is not only able to command premium prices, but look price shoppers in the face and tell them he's the most expensive store in the county. And he lands many of those sales. He also instantly snatches away the price shopper's biggest weapon. If she says he's too expensive, he says, "Yup, we're the most expensive in town. We're probably not the right store for you."

What else is the prospect going to say? She's just fired her biggest gun and the bullet bounced off Jimmy's chest.

And it gets even better. By first telling the prospect that he's the most expensive, and then following it up with "We probably won't be able to help you," Jimmy is subtly letting the prospect know that if she doesn't buy from Jimmy, she's proving that she's a cheapskate. Jimmy has turned the prospect's implied insult that "you're not worth the price you're asking" right back on her. Brilliant!

How would it feel to do the same thing with prospects who try to beat *you* up on price? How would it feel to be able to command premium prices? Empowering? Fun? Exhilarating? Liberating? Yup. I've done this in my businesses, and the feeling is amazing. The online strategies in this book are designed to differentiate you from all the other dealers in your market, and make it easy to command margins of 45% or more. You've just got to implement them. We can help you. Check out the materials shipped with this book, or visit **FloorDealerSuccess.com.**

# Florida Dealer Only Works 4 Days Per week, and His Revenue is Way Up!

Before I met Craig, he was working 60+ hours per week. "I used to work 'dark to dark,' including weekends," He told me. "The stress was terrible."

Craig is a dealer from Florida who grew up in the business. His family has been in the flooring business since the mid 1950's, and in 1975 they moved to Florida and opened a store. He started out at the age of 12, sweeping the floor and mowing the lawn, moving on to warehouse management and scheduling installers. In 2004 he went into sales, and eventually took over as owner in 2011.

"I focused on the minutiae of the business like selling, closing, getting the measurements right, nylon vs. polyester," Craig said. "I hadn't thought about all the stuff that comes at you as an owner like cash flow, advertising details, or sales people showing up out of the blue."

During his first year as owner, Craig stayed on the sales floor handling sales tasks, as well as bookkeeping and all the other responsibilities. He soon found himself falling further and further behind. "A flooring manager and I used to joke that we worked dark to dark," Craig said. "The hours didn't matter, I never looked at a clock, it was just dark to dark. I worked six or seven days a week, 60-plus hours a week. My margins were low and my stress was high."

That's when Craig saw my column in *Floor Covering News*, and inquired about my program.

Within 12 months Craig was working far fewer hours. "I show up each day at 10:00 a.m., I leave by 5:00, and I take Fridays, Saturdays and Sundays off," Craig said. He only works four days per week, less than 30 hours weekly. This is something most dealers only dream of.

Craig's revenue and margins are up, and his stress levels are down. Not only is he working less, he's making a lot more money. After joining my program, his revenue went up 50% two years in a row! He is able to afford a great in-store team which allows him to work the hours *he* chooses. He and his wife take vacations, and he's no longer shackled to his store.

Not long after implementing these changes in his business, Craig had lunch with a fellow flooring dealer in his town who was new to the business. "As usual, we placed our cell phones on the table in case we got a call," Craig told me. "Mine didn't ring once, but the other guy's cell never stopped. He talked to his installers twice, the salesperson once, handling all the picky little details himself, interrupted some 10-20 times in the course of two hours. No one at my store needed me. It practically runs itself now. But my friend was totally stressed out. He couldn't even get away from his business for two hours without constant interruptions."

Which dealer do you most resemble right now? Craig, who is able to leave his business for hours, days or weeks at a time and it runs without him? Or his friend who can't even go to lunch without 20 interruptions? If you're more like Craig's friend, there is hope. You can have the lifestyle you've always dreamed of. You can step into the kind of life Craig has, and it begins with implementing the strategies in this book.

The best part? We can implement them for you. Check out the materials shipped with this book, or visit **FloorDealerSuccess.com.**

# DEALER COMMENTS

### EXPONENTIAL GROWTH FOR FLOOR DEALERS

"The techniques that Jim is teaching, and the systems that he's looking to put in place for the average dealer are sure to work if they're executed properly. He's got a great blueprint for people to be much more successful without making a sizeable investment. In our industry there's a lot of training on product knowledge and salesmanship; there's a lot of great stuff out there. But what Jim does is take it a step further. He teaches dealers how to take what they're already doing and get the kind of exponential growth that no one thinks is possible."

- Scott Perron, President of 24/7 Floors and Floors 4 Pros

(Former President of Big Bob's Flooring)

"We've been emailing the eNeighborhood Advisor for a while, but we were a bit skeptical about spending the money to send out the printed copy of the Neighborhood Advisor. Well, the first paper copy started landing in peoples' mailboxes last Friday. On Monday, I had a client come in based on the newsletter – her job alone will pay for the whole mailing for the month, and then some.

We have had someone come in based on the newsletter or insert each day this week, including people who have shopped with us before but not made a purchase. The vast majority of our clients have responded really well to it – in month two, it's already starting to get traction."

- Matt Capell, ID

"Dear Jim, My residential jobs are booked solid for 6 weeks, and commercial jobs for 2 months! I also made $13,000 with one strategy that only cost $50. I'm getting great feedback from customers about your World Class Installation System! Thanks for everything, Jim!
-Jerry Johnson, TX

"My annual revenue went from $240,000 to $800,000 in 18 months thanks to Jim's systems!"
-Joe Hemphill, CO

X

**JIM, WE ARE GETTING READY TO HIRE MORE OFFICE HELP AND 2 MORE INSTALLATION CREWS.** *"We have been booked out with work 3 weeks for the last 4 months. When I look back a year and a half ago wondering how I was going to afford to pay you to join your program, WOW what a difference today is. I don't think I would be in business today if not for all your input and help, keep up the great coaching. Business is going GREAT profits and sales are up thanks to you. My margins are at 50% across the board. Just wanted to take a minute out of my busy life to say THANKS!*

*- Garry Combs, Illinois*

**I FEEL LIKE I'M FINALLY OFF THE ROLLER COASTER.**

*"I get compliments about the Neighborhood Advisor and eNeighborhood Advisor all the time. People love to receive them! We really want to make our clients feel like a part of the family, and the newsletters are a big part of that. It's helped a lot with referrals, too. It feels like we've finally gotten off the roller coaster of up and down business. In fact, now we're booked out at least three weeks at all times!"*
*- Shari Szymanski, WI*

**$100,000 ROI FROM THE *NEIGHBORHOOD ADVISOR***

*"The Neighborhood Advisor connects me to the community and makes me kind of a celebrity, and I get recognized - even just going out to lunch. Someone stopped me at Panera today for lunch to say hello. The Neighborhood Advisor makes me more than a company or a business. [Plus I've seen] $100,000 in ROI just from the Neighborhood Advisor."*

*- Paul Gardiner, NY*

*"I Made $64,779.64 from the Neighborhood Advisor in one month!"*

*-Marty Kiser, TN*

*"I made an extra $90,463 in one month using Jim's strategies."*
*-David Kocian, TX*

XI

**I'M TAKING WEEKENDS OFF TO TRAVEL WITH MY WIFE...IT'S FINALLY HAPPENING FOR ME!** *"I was working 70 or more hours a week, including weekends, and feeling incredibly burned out and, frankly, discouraged. I saw the successes of other dealers in cutting their hours and getting control of their business, and it was frustrating but also inspiring. I'm happy to say that, because of what I learned, this Summer I'm taking weekends to travel and spend time with my wife; the stress has dropped immensely. It's finally happened for me! I believe that every business owner should invest the time and money to go through the program. You can easily get the savings back in time and money."*

*- Curt Bowler, MT*

**WE NEEDED A WAY TO ADVERTISE THAT WAS DIFFERENT FROM WHAT EVERYONE ELSE WAS DOING!** *"I wanted more training for my sales staff. As a store, we've always catered to the middle and upper-tier client. We're more expensive than other stores, and I wanted the best approach for our clients. We really wanted to grow the business more and potentially continue expanding, so we needed a way to advertise that was different from what everyone else was doing. The principles of the Design Audit have been perfect for that. Flooring Success Systems has given us the ability to promote ourselves as the best." -Kathie Rice, FL*

**MY WIFE AND I WENT TO CABO... OUR FIRST VACATION IN YEARS!**

*"Our big challenge was we were growing quickly with our foot on the gas, but did not have the systems in place to properly take our business to the next level. I was working 7 days per week just to keep up. Through Jim's program I've been able to implement systems so I can delegate, and have the peace of mind that things are getting handled correctly without me there to babysit. As a result, I've cut my work hours so I can take weekends off. Also my wife and I went on vacation to Cabo. It was our first vacation in years. The stress relief is unbelievable." - Jay Robinson, VA*

*"I stopped wasting $15,000 - $20,000 per month on advertising...And My Sales Went Up! Thanks, Jim!"*

*- Tim Rea, MN*

*"I'm working less than 30 hours per week, revenue is up 50%... Business is fun again!"*

*-Earl Swalm, SK*

*"The Design Audit has been great for us. With over 10,000 products in our store, clients can get very overwhelmed. Now, we get them to the table as soon as possible to have a conversation about their needs. It really puts people at ease, and lets us position ourselves as consultants. The Design Audit lets us make the experience easy and hassle-free for people. We come to them with the two products that are going to be best for them, instead of leaving them to wander through our inventory feeling confused and overwhelmed. Cash flow is really good right now – we've improved our close rates and we're able to focus on the clients who are in our desired client profile."*

*-Dave Federici, NJ*

*"...I've Made Over $250,000 In Extra Income...So Far!"*

*- Brent B, UT*

*"We love having Home Depot as our neighbor! We take a lot of business from them!*

*-Mark Bouquet, IL (That's Mark In The Photo)*

*I've only been a member for three months, but because of Jim's systems I've raised my prices 30%...I'm now getting no less than 50% margins on everything I sell. And I'm even busier than before I raised my prices! Thanks, Jim!"*

*-Garry & Cindy Combs, IL*

*"My revenue has doubled and tripled."*

*-Steve D'Angelo, AZ*

*"Our Revenue Is Up 79.3% Over Last Year! Thanks, Jim!"*

*-Mike Phoenix, CT*

*"Jim, I just wanted you to know that had I not joined AND PUT IT ON A CREDIT CARD, I would have been a statistic. But with the growth of the retail, and the connection, we have been able to carry somehow these massive jobs. So when I say thank you, I want you to know that I believe you were a Godsend. I wish nothing but the best for you and yours Jim. God bless You my Friend,"*

*-Mark Bouquet, IL*

*"P.S. I am going to make a prediction that we will do 4 to 5 million this coming year!"*

*"Costa Rica! Blended drinks on the beach with my Bride of 25 plus years, Carolyn. We had a blast! This was our first vacation in 8 years. Jim, thanks for the motivation to let our store work for us rather than us working for the store."*

*-Dan Ginnaty, MT*

# DON'T ENVY THESE DEALERS ... JOIN THEM!

Check out the information shipped with this book, or visit FloorDealerSuccess.com.

# WHAT FLOORING INDUSTRY LEADERS ARE SAYING ABOUT JIM AUGUSTUS ARMSTRONG

**WORLD FLOOR COVERING ASSOCIATION**

**~Scott Humphrey**
*CEO, World Floor Covering Association*

"True leadership is found in action. I very much appreciate the leadership shown by Jim Armstrong through his FcNews Marketing Mastery Webinars. We have been blessed to guest several times through different branches of the WFCA. He and his team have handled all of the promotions and set up. The process could not have been easier. If you want the opportunity to partner effortlessly with a leader who is committed to amplifying your voice, you want to partner with Jim!"

**~John Mcgrath**
*Executive Director, INSTALL*

"I've attended Jim's webinars, and he is an excellent speaker. There's a lot of good training out there, but what I appreciate about Jim is he gives flooring retailers strategies that are very practical, and can have a measurable impact if they are implemented. I've also been a guest on the Marketing Mastery Webinars that he co-hosts, and he worked very hard to make the event a success. He interviewed me beforehand to get a good grasp of the topic, and provided promotional emails to send to my list, and took care of all the details. I wholeheartedly recommend Jim for speaking and training."

**~Tom Jennings**
*WFCA, Vice President of Professional Development*

"Jim Augustus Armstrong does an excellent job providing flooring retailers with relevant strategies that work. I have found him to be an engaging speaker who cares about helping retailers succeed. Twice I've been a guest on the Marketing Mastery Webinars Jim hosts for Floor Covering News. Both events were handled in a very professional manner. I highly recommend Jim to speak at your next event."

**~Jennifer Hughes**
*Education Manager, Informa Global
Exhibitions (Surfaces)*

"Jim Augustus Armstrong has spoken at The International Surface Event for several years. His sessions have been well-attended, and they receive positive comments from attendees. He and his team are very professional and easy to work with. I highly recommend Jim for speaking and training."

**~Robert Varden**
*Vice President, CFI Division of WFCA*

"I've attended Jim Augustus Armstrong's trainings, and he is an engaging speaker, and provides real nuts-and-bolts strategies that floor dealers can incorporate into their businesses easily. I've also been a guest speaker on the Marketing Mastery Webinars Jim produces for Floor Covering News. He makes it very convenient for me to participate because he handles all the set up and promotions. I highly recommend Jim for speaking at your events."

# floor covering news

**~Dustin Aaronson**
*Associate Publisher/Co-owner, FCNews*

"I have known Jim Augustus Armstrong since 2007 through his partnership with FCNews. He writes our Marketing Mastery column, and he developed and produces our monthly Marketing Mastery Webinars. Our readers appreciate his training because it's relevant, and they can put his strategies to work immediately in their businesses. Also, Jim and his team do a great job handling all the marketing and promotions for the webinars. If you're considering hiring Jim to speak, he will do a fantastic job, and bring tremendous value to your attendees. He and his team can also help promote, which is a big plus. Feel free to contact me directly with any questions."